THE
DOOLITTLE
RAIDERS

GEORGE NOLTA

THE DOOLITTLE RAIDERS

What Heroes Do after the War

4880 Lower Valley Road • Atglen, PA 19310

Dedication
Ellen Reynolds Lawson (1919–2009)
"Collector Extraordinaire"

"The bravest are surely those who have the clearest vision of what is before them, glory and danger alike, and yet notwithstanding go out to meet it."

Cover design by John Cheek
Interior design by Matt Goodman
Type set in PF Din Display Pro, PF Din Mono, PF Din Condensed, Minion Pro.

All black-and-white photographs were provided courtesy of World War II Database—founded and edited by C. Peter Chen of Lava Development, LLC. All colorized photos provided through courtesy of Lori Lang of LBL Graphic Design. Copyright © 2017 Lori Lang, LBL Graphic Design. All Rights Reserved.

ISBN: 978-0-7643-5614-8

Printed in China

Published by Schiffer Publishing, Ltd.
4880 Lower Valley Road
Atglen, PA 19310
Phone: (610) 593-1777; Fax: (610) 593-2002
E-mail: Info@schifferbooks.com
Web: www.schifferbooks.com

For our complete selection of fine books on this and related subjects, please visit our website at www.schifferbooks.com. You may also write for a free catalog.

Schiffer Publishing's titles are available at special discounts for bulk purchases for sales promotions or premiums. Special editions, including personalized covers, corporate imprints, and excerpts, can be created in large quantities for special needs. For more information, contact the publisher.

We are always looking for people to write books on new and related subjects. If you have an idea for a book, please contact us at proposals@schifferbooks.com.

Contents

Foreword

The first bombing raid on Japan during World War II was on April 18, 1942. Sixteen B-25s with five crew members each carried out this secret mission under the capable leadership of aviation expert Jimmy Doolittle. This is the rest of the story about those eighty United States Air Corps men, now best known as "Doolittle Tokyo Raiders."

Their names, with next of kin with addresses, were listed in the postscript section of *Thirty Seconds over Tokyo*, written by my husband, Capt. Ted Lawson, edited by Bob Considine, and published by Random House, initially in 1943. When C. V. Glines published his *Doolittle Tokyo Raiders* in 1964, all the Raiders were again listed, with a short summary of each man plus the decorations they had received.

After attending the fiftieth anniversary of the Doolittle Raiders in 1992, it was obvious that too-many years had passed without learning more about these men. There was lots of encouragement from my family, friends, and so many others showing interest to write about my unusual life, married for fifty-plus years to Ted Lawson. I decided to name this yet-to-be-written book *Out of the Blue*.

Our first assignment was to McChord Field, Washington, in 1941 with the 17th Bomb Group. Here, after Pearl Harbor, many of the pilots were on submarine patrol over the Pacific and became good friends and also volunteered for the mission. In 1995, after having started the book *Out of the Blue*, the chapter about the Raider family was in need of help. Letters were mailed to the then-living Raiders asking for biographies and stories. The result turned out to be too much for one chapter of *Out of the Blue*, so with the help of George Nolta, the material became this book.

Ellen Lawson
October 2007

Preface

Much has been written about the famous Doolittle Raid on Japan, and the eighty brave crew members who flew the near-suicidal mission from the deck of the USS *Hornet* to the heartland of Japan. However, very little has been written about the lives of these men after the war ended and the excitement of the war years faded into the history books. Many books were written about different Raiders' experiences as they flew the mission and evaded the Japanese search through China. However, little is known about these men as they passed through the after-war years and entered retirement. Ellen Lawson decided to take up the challenge of recording something about the Raiders as they passed through the remaining phases of their lives. Ellen was married to Maj. Ted Lawson, one of the Raiders and author of the now-classic *Thirty Seconds over Tokyo*. Ellen was an inveterate collector of Raider memorabilia, and it was quite easy for her to take on the task of collecting biographies, news clippings, obituaries, and various other kinds of documentation about the post-Raid lives of the Raiders. She started this collection in 1942 and always had the intention to share the information with family and friends of the Raiders. As an extra bonus to the collection of information about the eighty veterans of the Raid, some of the Raiders or their families have provided journals or diaries of their Raid experiences, which greatly enhance the other life-story information.

I felt proud and privileged to pull all this information together and to organize and write a book that will complete more of this story for historical reference. This collection phase was a long but happy experience for Ellen and is a tribute to the brave men of the Doolittle Raid. This collection also is a tribute to the consideration and sensitivity of such a wonderful lady, who served as unofficial historian of the post-Raid Raiders. Ellen made this collection available to me and asked me to organize it into a book that could be shared with the families and fans of the Raiders. As I digested and sorted the various pieces of information, I supplemented them with fresh Internet research, as well as input from various Raider family members who volunteered corrections and additions. While not intended as full biographies, it is hoped that the review of each crew member's biographical sketch can give a flavor of his life's path after the war.

As a grammar school kid in Willows, California, in the late 1940s, I had the unique opportunity to meet Gen. Doolittle. He and a group of friends were visiting my uncles Floyd "Speed" Nolta and Dale Nolta on one of Doolittle's many hunting trips. Jimmy and Floyd had served together in the army air corps at Rockwell Field in San Diego during World War I and remained lifelong friends. I couldn't comprehend at the time the significance of this great man and his brave crews. I do now. There were sixteen B-25s that took off from the deck of the USS *Hornet* on April 18, 1942. Each carried a crew of five: pilot, copilot, navigator, bombardier, and flight engineer/gunner. This book is divided into sixteen chapters—one for each crew—in the same sequence that they took off from the *Hornet*. It will take you from where they were born to where they died, with a few stops in between.

George A. Nolta
June 2017

Introduction

Americans were shocked and demoralized when hundreds of Japanese fighter, bomber, and torpedo planes made their surprise attack at Pearl Harbor on December 7, 1941. This event dragged our isolationist country into the Second World War. Two weeks after the attack, President Franklin D. Roosevelt quickly ordered his top military advisors to develop a plan for a retaliatory strike on mainland Japan. He wanted to prove to the Japanese leaders that they did not enjoy an impregnable position, and he wanted to give a morale-building boost to the American people. A ground invasion or a naval bombardment was not possible, due to the strong defensive perimeter around the Japanese fortress, as well as the long distance from the US mainland and the relatively weak status of the US military at the time. An aerial bombing seemed like the best prospect, but America lacked the long-range bombers for such an attack, and aircraft carriers could not get close enough to Japan to launch their typically small planes. So what to do?

A surprise compromise became the answer. Two naval staff officers came up with the creative idea and a basic plan detailing how slightly modified army twin-engine bombers could take off from a navy aircraft carrier beyond the Japanese defensive perimeter. The North American B-25 Mitchell bomber was the only medium-range plane in the American arsenal that fit the narrow window of acceptance—enough bomb-carrying capacity and range to make the flight over Japan and on into the safety of China, but small enough to be carried and launched from a carrier. The initial idea for the Raid was the brainchild of navy captain Francis Low, who was a brilliant submariner with a history of bold creativity. He took the idea to Adm. Ernest King, who was both commander in chief of the US fleet and the chief of naval operations. Seeing the great possibility, he refined it with Capt. Donald "Wu" Duncan, his aviation expert. They in turn took the proposal to army chief of staff Gen. Henry H. "Hap" Arnold. Gen. Arnold approved it, and he picked Lt. Col. Jimmy Doolittle to plan and lead the attack—and so was born the "Doolittle Raid on Japan."

On the basis of secret tests on the USS *Hornet*, the navy quickly confirmed that a B-25 could take off from an aircraft carrier, assuming the carrier was moving fast enough and that there was sufficient headwind. Unfortunately, the B-25s could not land back on the carrier due to various design factors, such as their high landing speed and their lack of airframe strength in the tail section for a tail hook. Col. Doolittle set about the task of planning and testing the feasibility of several modifications to the B-25. The most significant change was the design and installation of extra fuel tanks. The planes would need to carry much extra fuel to handle the long flight to and over Japan and then on into mainland China. The plan was to land at friendly air bases in China and turn the B-25s over to the Chinese to use in their fight with the Japanese. The seaboard of China was occupied and controlled by the Japanese, so Doolittle's planes would have to fly farther inland to find free China bases.

Doolittle determined that most of his needed volunteer crew members could come from the 34th, 37th, and 95th squadrons of the 17th Bombardment Group, and its associated Reconnaissance Squadron (under Maj. John A. "Jack" Hilger), all stationed at Pendleton Field, Oregon. Those men had already been trained in the B-25, and some had extensive flying experience with it while patrolling for enemy submarines along the Oregon and Washington coast. He picked an interim training base at Columbia Army Air Base in Columbia, South Carolina, with the final training base at Eglin Field, in the western Florida Panhandle. Much of the training involved practicing short takeoffs, but it also involved day and night navigation, gunnery, bombing, and formation flying.

In his book *I Could Never Be So Lucky Again*, Doolittle said: "My plane was to leave first about three hours ahead of everybody else, with the remaining fifteen planes divided into five flights of three planes each. Each flight was assigned a course, and then each plane had specific targets within the flight's general area. We planned to spread the mission over a fifty-mile front in order to create the impression that a larger number of planes took part in the raid than were actually used, and to dilute enemy air and ground fire. This also negated the possibility of more than one plane passing over any given point on the ground and assured an element of surprise."

The five flights were assigned as follows:

1. The first, led by Lt. Travis Hoover, was to cover the northern part of Tokyo.
2. The second, led by Capt. Davey Jones, was to cover southern Tokyo.
3. The third, led by Capt. Ski York, was to cover the southern part of Tokyo and the north-central part of the Tokyo Bay area.
4. The fourth, led by Capt. Ross Greening, was to cover the southern part of Kanagawa, the city of Yokohama, and the Yokosuka navy yard.
5. The fifth, led by Maj. Jack Hilger, was to go around southern Tokyo, proceed to Nagoya, and then split up, with one plane bombing Nagoya, one bombing Osaka, and one bombing Kobe.

The planes were to be transported from the Alameda Naval Air Station to the launch site by Task Force 16, composed of the carrier *Hornet* plus fourteen other ships, all commanded by Adm. William "Bull" Halsey. Doolittle instructed that once the planes took off from the *Hornet*, everyone was on his own and nobody was to fly in formation. There was to be no radio communication of any kind, in order to ensure complete surprise and personal safety. The planes were to fly at extremely low altitude to avoid Japanese radar. The plan was to launch about 400 miles from Japan, bomb their targets, then fly on to the safe sites in China. Unfortunately, the American armada spotted some Japanese vessels well before the launch point, and the naval commanders feared that their location would be communicated to the Japanese mainland. As a result, Adm. Halsey ordered the planes to launch early—about 800 miles from Tokyo. In his book *Not as Briefed*, Col. C. Ross Greening said: "We were 800 miles from Japan—twice the distance we had bargained for, and 200 more miles more than what was considered really feasible for the amount of fuel we carried." This meant they could not reach their safe landing sites. With this quick stroke of fate, the Raid became a virtual suicide mission. With insufficient fuel to reach the safe bases in interior China, the Raiders faced the prospect of crashing at sea or bailing out over Japanese-held territory. Knowing the risk involved, Doolittle quickly surveyed his men and offered the option for anyone to decline to go on the mission. Not a single man accepted the offer.

The Raid took place on April 18, 1942, just four short months after Pearl Harbor. It was the first airstrike on the Japanese homeland in World War II. All sixteen planes dropped their bomb load and made it safely out of Japan. The closest free China airfield was at Chuchow, which was about 1,200 miles from Japan. At a gas-saving speed of 150 mph, this escape route was about an eight-hour journey. An unexpected tailwind barely gave them the ability to reach the Chinese mainland, or else they all would have crash-landed in the East China Sea with little hope of survival. Fifteen of the planes reached China, but they had no place to land, so the crews either bailed out over land or else rode their plane into an ocean crash landing. One crew decided to take their plane to a safe landing in Vladivostok in the Soviet Union, where they were interned for a little over a year. Of the eighty crew members:

- One man was killed on bailout.
- Two men drowned as a result of crash-landing in the water off the China coast.
- Eight men were captured by the Japanese. Of these, three were executed by firing squad, one died of illness, and the other four survived forty months of prison.
- Five men were interned in Russia for thirteen months until they escaped across the border into Persia (now Iran).
- The other sixty-four survived the Raid, escaped through China, and returned to service, although some sustained serious injuries.

The Raid did some physical damage but did not do the kind of damage that occurred later in the war with the devastating B-29 fire bombings of Japan. Perhaps the most-significant effects of the Raid were the psychological impacts both on the Japanese and American people. American morale got a significant boost with such a quick and successful raid, and the Japanese learned that they were not invulnerable to attack in their island fortress. In addition, the Japanese relocated a number of military assets because of the Raid, and they recalled many military units back to their mainland for defense. Many historians believe this weakened the Japanese offensive posture in Asia and the Pacific, which contributed to their significant naval loss at the Battle of Midway two months later in June 1942.

Many interesting books and movies have been made about the Raid and the escape through China. One of the first to get published was Ted Lawson's *Thirty Seconds over Tokyo*. Ted collaborated on the book with Robert "Bob" Considine while he was recovering from serious injuries in Walter Reed Hospital. The book was made into a classic movie, starring Spencer Tracy as Jimmy Doolittle, Van Johnson as Ted Lawson, and Phyllis Thaxter as Ellen Lawson. Some of the other interesting books about the Raid are listed in the bibliography.

The healthy survivors quickly got back into the war—some staying to fly in the Far East, and others flying in Europe and North Africa. Some flyers were killed in action later in the war, some were captured and became prisoners of war, and some stayed in the air force after the war as a career. Many went on to interesting and varied careers in the private sector. Of those who stayed in the air force as a career, five rose to the rank of general: James Doolittle, John Hilger, Davey M. Jones, Everett Holstrom, and Richard Knobloch. This collection of biographical sketches attempts to amplify the lives and careers of the Raiders before and after the Raid.

Acknowledgments

The core of this book is based on a unique collection of Raider facts and memorabilia collected by Ellen Lawson over a fifty-plus-year period. Ellen was the wife of Maj. Ted Lawson—pilot of plane #7 and author of *Thirty Seconds over Tokyo*. Ellen and Ted settled in my hometown of Chico, California, for their retirement years. I wrote an article about Ellen in 2005 for the Colusi County Historical Society, and we became friends. She asked me to write a book about the Raiders, on the basis of her collection of information. Some of the material in this book has been copied verbatim from correspondence and newspaper clippings and summaries provided by the veterans or their family members over many years, and I have borrowed heavily from various books on the Raid. Some of the crew members left a broad footprint of documented activities as they journeyed through life. Others almost disappeared from view, and there were few scraps found to document their life. Due to the informal nature of the collection, no attempt has been made to quote or give credit to every single source, so thanks is given to all those who have generously contributed.

Many members of "Children of the Doolittle Raiders" made significant additions and corrections to my first draft. Raider family members who contributed were Gabrielle Adelman, Jim Barnett, Casey Blanton, James Bower, John Campbell, Rich Cole, Carolyn Spatz Davidson, Carol Dixon, Michael Emmens, Gary Griffin, Chuck Greening, Susan K. Hoffman, Todd Joyce, Sandra Knobloch, Herb Macia, Bob Parker, Jeff Thatcher, Carolyn Ward, and Constance B. Townsend.

This book would not have been possible without the help of many other generous people who gave of their time and knowledge. I would particularly like to thank the late C. V. Glines, who helped considerably with the initial review of my first draft. In addition, Dee March provided a valuable service to do genealogical research, which was the key to overcoming several brick walls. Significant information was gathered from Todd Joyce's impressive website at www.doolittleraider.com. Much additional information was garnered via the electronic magic of the Internet.

Gene Russell, EdD, played an essential role in proofreading my drafts and correcting my numerous editorial shortcomings. Cliff Larimer—a semiretired peripatetic newspaperman from Willows, California—also provided some much-needed editing. A final review by Bob Fish—a trustee of the USS *Hornet* Museum—corrected errors that helped improve the book.

Crew No. 1

Pilot.................Lt. Col. James H. Doolittle
Copilot.......................Lt. Richard E. Cole
Navigator.....................Lt. Henry A. Potter
Bombardier..................S.Sgt. Fred A. Braemer
Flight Engineer/Gunner......S.Sgt. Paul J. Leonard

JAMES HAROLD DOOLITTLE
Pilot

Pre-Raid

Jimmy was born on December 14, 1896, in Alameda, California. He attended Los Angeles Junior College in 1916–17, before enrolling at the University of California, Berkeley, in the School of Mines. At the time, he was aiming for a degree in mining engineering. When the United States entered World War I in 1917, Jimmy enlisted in the Aviation Section of the Army's Signal Corps without finishing college. He was assigned back to Berkeley for aviation ground school, where he finished training and received his commission as second lieutenant in March 1918. He married Josephine "Jo" Daniels on Christmas Eve 1917.

In his early days, Jimmy was a little impulsive and overaggressive in his flying. In her book *Calculated Risk*, Jimmy's granddaughter Jonna Doolittle Hoppes tells us about one of Jimmy's embarrassing incidents when he was a young instructor pilot at Rockwell Field in San Diego in 1918. The army air corps was pushing its pilots to set new flying records to help promote the flying service and improve the flying budgets. Jimmy suggested to his commanding officer—Lt. Col. Harry Burwell—that he and two other pilots fly three Jennys from San Diego to Washington, DC, to demonstrate how fast mail and personnel could be transported from coast to coast. Burwell surprisingly approved the idea in spite of several unfavorable earlier experiences with Doolittle's unauthorized flying stunts. Unfortunately, all three Jennys crash-landed while getting no farther than Arizona, so the demonstration failed. Jimmy climbed out of his plane, snagging his pants on the cockpit and ripping a flap in the seat. He rushed back to base to face Burwell's anger. Burwell chewed him out for poor planning, and Jimmy knew it was true. As he turned to leave, the torn flap on his pants hung open to expose his hindquarters. Livid, and taking the exposure as an implied insult, Burwell's anger exploded with "Doolittle, you're so stupid you can't even keep your ass in your pants!"

Jimmy belatedly received his BS degree from the University of California in 1922, and then his MS degree from the Massachusetts Institute of Technology in 1924. The following year, he received his doctor-of-science degree in aeronautical engineering from MIT.

So much has been written about Jimmy Doolittle's outstanding career that there is little need to duplicate it here, except for some key highlights. He was a barnstormer, a prize-winning air racer, and overachieving pilot. Jimmy was handpicked by Gen. "Hap" Arnold to engineer a plan for attacking Japan with medium bombers taking off from an aircraft carrier—a feat that had never been done before. Gen. Arnold never intended for Doolittle to lead the Raid, since

Jimmy was playing an influential role on Arnold's staff in Washington, DC. However, Jimmy begged and wheedled permission from Arnold to lead the Raid that he had so carefully planned. The final training for the mission took place at Eglin Field in Florida. As the crews were finishing their short-takeoff training at Eglin, the USS *Hornet* was making its way through the Panama Canal, headed for the San Francisco Bay area. Naval commanders were working with Adm. Chester Nimitz's staff at Pearl Harbor to prepare the navy's role in the Raid. When the navy was ready for Doolittle to move his crews from Eglin to the *Hornet* at Alameda Naval Air Station, the navy wired a cryptic seven-word message to Adm. King in Washington, then to Gen. Arnold, then to Doolittle. The message simply read: "TELL JIMMY TO GET ON HIS HORSE." Doolittle released his crews to start the first leg of their historic mission by flying cross-country to the Sacramento Air Depot (later renamed McClelland Field) for final engine tuning, and then on to Alameda for boarding the *Hornet*. The crews were directed to fly individually so as not to attract attention, and to practice their low-level navigation, which they thoroughly enjoyed because legal "hedgehopping" was a rare but fun experience.

Post-Raid

Jimmy's B-25 was the first over Japan and the first to drop its bomb load. His four incendiaries fell at 12:30 p.m. Tokyo time to ignite a large factory. Doolittle then flew to reach the coast of China after dark. By 9:30 p.m., fuel was low and they were unable to find an airfield in the heavy fog. Jimmy ordered his crew to bail out among the mountains of China near Tian Mushem, about 70 miles north of Chuchow. Local Chinese escorted the crew to Chuchow, and then on to Chunking. Doolittle initially thought his mission was a failure, since they had been unable to complete the second half of the mission—to deliver the bombers to American units then being formed in China. He was genuinely surprised in Chunking when Gen. Arnold wired congratulations on his promotion from lieutenant colonel to brigadier general, skipping the rank of colonel.

Doolittle was quietly whisked back to Washington, where Gen. Arnold and Gen. George C. Marshall, then army chief of staff, escorted him to the White House, where President Roosevelt presented him with the Medal of Honor. Later in 1942, Gen. Arnold recommended to Gen. Dwight D. Eisenhower, commander of American forces in England, that Doolittle be assigned to organize and command the 12th Air Force, which was being activated to invade North Africa and to carry the war to the Axis forces that were occupying the entire region. Jimmy flew twenty-five combat missions while commanding the 12th Air Force. He took over command of the 8th Air Force in January 1944 and was promoted to lieutenant general in March 1944. He then became the first US Army Reserve officer in history to attain three stars.

In her book *Calculated Risk*, Jonna Doolittle Hoppes relates this humorous anecdote: "Churchill declared May 8, 1945 to be V-E Day (Victory in Europe). Gen. George Patton and Gen. Doolittle received orders to tour the United States to bolster morale and raise needed funds for the completion of the war against Japan. One of their stops was in Los Angeles at the Coliseum. Accompanied by their wives, Doolittle and Patton took turns addressing the crowd. Jimmy said: 'If Gen. Patton and I have achieved any success in fighting the war, these two lovely ladies are responsible for that success because of their constant support, understanding and affection.' The crowd roared their approval with a standing ovation. Patton leaned over to Doolittle and a hot mic picked up Patton's casual comment and blasted it throughout the Coliseum: 'You son of a bitch, I wish I'd said that!'"

When the Germans surrendered in May 1945, Jimmy returned to the States and had a reunion with his wife, Jo, and his sons, James "Jim" Jr. and John, the latter of whom was a cadet at West Point. He learned that he would be moving the 8th Air Force to the Pacific. The new 8th Air Headquarters was officially opened at Okinawa on July 26, 1945, as Jimmy prepared for the arrival of men and planes from the States. However, the *"Enola Gay"* dropped the first atomic bomb on Hiroshima on August 6, 1945, and the 8th Air Force never saw combat against the Japanese. Jimmy attended the Japanese surrender ceremony on August 15 on the battleship *Missouri*.

Doolittle left active duty in the fall of 1945 and accepted a job with Shell Oil Company. He continued to serve on various military boards and commissions. In addition, he played key roles in various organizations, such as the Space Technologies Laboratories, TRW Systems, Mutual of Omaha Insurance Company, Aerospace Corporation, United Benefit Life, and others. In 1985, President Ronald Reagan awarded Jimmy with a fourth star—another unprecedented event for a reserve officer.

Jimmy's granddaughter Jonna wrote: "My grandfather retired from active service and went back into private industry. He served on numerous boards and as an advisor to every president from Truman through Kennedy. He never really retired but continued to keep an office up until two weeks before he passed away in 1993. His hobbies centered on hunting and fishing. He and my grandmother remained close to the Raiders and we grew up thinking of them as uncles. They called my grandfather 'Boss' or 'the Old Man' and my grandmother 'Momma Jo.' Although my grandfather went on to command the 12th Air Force, the 15th Air Force and the 8th Air Force in World War II, a part of his heart always belonged to his Raiders."

Jimmy and Jo had a very traumatic event in April 1958, when they got the shattering news that their thirty-eight-year-old son James Jr. had committed suicide. At the time, James Jr. was commander of the 524th Fighter-Bomber

Squadron at Bergstrom AFB, Austin, Texas. He left no note, so the family never knew for sure why he took his own life. His first marriage had ended in divorce, and he had recently been passed over for promotion. His fellow officers and his second wife had noticed that he had appeared despondent and depressed in the previous six weeks or so.

As a method to help deal with his grief, Jimmy took some time alone after the funeral to think some "philosophical thoughts," which he wrote down. Part of what he wrote was disclosed in his autobiography: "Only when someone very near and dear to one leaves does one appreciate the stark tragedy of death. Even then nature tends to cushion the initial shock, and the thought 'He is gone' does not carry the later realization of finality and permanence that comes only with the final indisputable understanding that 'we will never see him again.' I can think of no greater misfortune for parents than when a child dies out of sequence in the natural order. It is something that I don't think one ever fully recovers from. Fortunately for Jo and me, we had Jim Jr.'s son—'Double Junior' (James III), who is an Air Force colonel at this writing; young Jim's second wife Shirley and her son Eric; our son John—a career Air Force officer who retired as a colonel, and his wife Priscilla, their five children, and our great-grandchildren to sustain us over the years. As great as the loss was to us, Jo and I knew we had to go on living. We buried ourselves in our respective activities and maintained contact with our large circle of friends. We seldom talked about our loss, but we never got over it."

Jimmy never thought of himself as a bold pilot, even though he crashed a number of times and always escaped unscathed. He told C. V. Glines, "I have always tried to be conservative. I've always tried to do something new, but before exhibiting that new thing before the public, I practiced it again and again to be sure the hazard was minimized as much as possible. My calculations didn't always work out precisely, however. Otherwise, I wouldn't have had to jump out of an airplane three times to save my neck."

Glines asked Jimmy about his personal philosophy when Jimmy was ninety. He answered, "My philosophy of life is really quite simple. I believe every person has been put on this earth for just one purpose: to serve his fellow man. It doesn't matter how he does this. He can build a bridge, paint a picture, invent a laborsaving gadget, or run a gas station. The point is he should try to leave the earth a better place than he found it. If he does, his life will have been worthwhile. If he doesn't do what he can within his own limitations, he is destined to be unhappy." Doolittle was a happy man.

Jimmy's beloved wife, Jo, died on December 24, 1988, their seventy-first wedding anniversary, and was buried at Arlington National Cemetery. In his book *I Could Never Be So Lucky Again*, Jimmy made these poignant remarks about his end-of-life phase: "On December 24, 1988, after a stroke, followed by months of steady physical deterioration, my precious Jo passed away. It was our seventy-first wedding anniversary. She rests forever in Arlington National Cemetery, where I will join her one of these days. In February 1990, I moved to Pebble Beach, California, where my son John and his wife Priscilla built their dream house on the property Jo and I had bought in the 1940s. They had a large addition constructed that is now my final residence and office. As I watch the many bird species scramble for position to get the seed I put out each day, I realize my life has gone full circle. I'm home and I'm content." Jimmy died at age ninety-six on September 27, 1993, and is buried with Jo at Arlington.

RICHARD E. COLE
Copilot

Pre-Raid

Dick Cole was born on September 7, 1915, in Dayton, Ohio. He graduated from Steele High School in Dayton and completed two years at Ohio University in Athens before enlisting as a flying cadet in November 1940. He attended the civilian pilot training program at Wittenberg College night school in Springfield, Ohio, and received a private-pilot rating. Dick enlisted in the US Army in November 1940 and attended Parks Air College—Randolph and Kelly Flying Schools. He was commissioned a second lieutenant in July 1941 and assigned to the 34th Bomb Squadron, 17th Bombardment Group, at Pendleton, Oregon, where he started flying B-25s. After the group was transferred to Columbia, South Carolina, he volunteered for the secret mission. Dick was twenty-six at the time of the Raid.

A Japanese picket ship sighted the task force on their way to Japan, so the navy had to scramble the Raiders for an earlier-than-expected departure. In *War Stories II: Heroism in the Pacific*, Oliver North quotes Dick Cole's description of the surprise: "The first thing that we heard that morning was the guns going off from the cruiser that had spotted the picket ship. I was at breakfast when they started firing. And immediately we all put breakfast aside and ran up topside to see what was going on. Then, right away they announced over the PA system, 'Army personnel, man your planes!' I had to run back down to where my quarters were and get my gear. For those of us who flew with Jimmy, the name of the game was to get to the airplane before the old man did. I got there in time to help Fred Braemer and Paul Leonard pull the props through and make a walk-around check, and we were "air-available" when the boss came. There was a low overcast and the sea was running high enough where water was coming up over the bow. In fact, the area where we were got wet, and they had to put down some abrasive pads for some of the later airplanes because they were sliding back and forth on the deck. As far as whether or not we were going to make it off the deck, I didn't even think about it. We had done the same thing on a runway with not near as much headwind. I had no doubt about it. We were flying with the best pilot in the world and besides that, being a second lieutenant, I had to worry about flaps, landing gear—stuff like that."

Post-Raid

After the Raid, Cole remained in the China-Burma-India theater flying C-47s for Air Transport Command, Special Project 7 (the "Hump"), between India and China. During that time, Cole flew 120 missions. Dennis Okerstrom's *Dick Cole's War* reported that when Dick was flying a C-47 into Burma on October 18, 1942, he noticed a plume of thick black smoke from the jungle, which indicated either a plane crash or a bomb strike on a fuel depot. As he drew closer, over the dense jungle with no roads or river, he confirmed that it was not smoke from a fuel dump. As he flew closer to investigate, he saw the broken swath of trees and a blackened hole in the tree canopy that confirmed a plane crash. At the completion of the mission, he learned that the crash site was the wreckage of a B-25 piloted by Lt. Robert Gray—pilot of the third Raider bomber. Also killed in the crash was Sgt. George Larkin Jr.—flight engineer of the tenth Raider bomber. The cause of the crash was never learned.

Upon returning to the States in summer of 1943, he was sent to Tulsa, Oklahoma, for duty as acceptance test pilot at the Douglas Aircraft plant. In September, he met Martha Harrell when she requested a ride on one of his test flights. Son Richard told me what happened next:

"Dad turned down her request for a ride as he was doing his walk-around inspection of the aircraft. He turned her down because it was a test flight. Dad completed his walk-around, got in, started the engines, and took off. On the climb out, Mom saunters up to the cockpit—somehow she had been able to sneak on as a stowaway. Dad aborted the flight. The copilot had a reputation as a ladies' man, and he asked Mom to write her number down on a matchbook cover. Mom wrote her number down on the matchbook cover but didn't give it to the copilot—she gave it to Dad. It took Dad a week to get up the nerve to call her for a date—his first date ever. They were married two weeks later.

After flying for Douglas for a short time, Dick volunteered for duty with the 1st Air Commando Group for Special Project 9, commanded by Col. Phil Cochran, Col. John Alison, and Gen. Orde Wingate in their campaign to drive the Japanese out of Burma. Dick returned to Burma in October 1943 and flew over 150 missions in the C-47 for the 1st Air Commandos and completed his tour in July 1944. He returned to Tulsa and resumed test flying at the Douglas plant.

In June 1945, Dick and Martha had their first child—Cindy. In the fall of 1946, Dick left the army air corps and entered Oregon State College in Corvallis. However, in July 1947, Cole was recalled to active duty, receiving a regular commission with assignment to Wright-Patterson AFB, Ohio. During this tour, the second daughter, Christina, arrived. In 1952, Dick was transferred to the Armed Forces Staff School at Norfolk, Virginia. While there, their third child arrived—Richard. After staff school, it was off to Japan and Korea to fly combat cargo and administrative missions until 1955, and then back stateside to the Pentagon until 1959. During this tour, the fourth child was born in 1956—Samuel, and then Andrew in 1958. A tour to Caracas, Venezuela, was next, followed with a final transfer to George AFB at Victorville in California. He retired in 1967 at the rank of lieutenant colonel.

Retirement took the Coles to a 20-acre citrus grove in Alamo, Texas, where they built a 4,000-square-foot home and started raising citrus and avocados until 1976. The farm was sold, and the family moved to Canyon Lake, where they built another home. This lake home was sold in 1980, and a move to San Antonio took place. Another house was built and they lived there until 1993, when they sold again and moved to the Texas hill country just outside Comfort, Texas.

Dick's military legacy continues. His oldest son, Richard, served in the air force, flying F-4s and F-15s. One of his grandsons—Nathan Chal—a graduate of the Air Force Academy, class of 2006, is currently flying the KC-135. In the May 2006 edition of the *Academy Spirit*, Nathan reflected on the flying legacy he inherited from his grandfather. Nathan said, "For the most part, Pops was, and is, extremely humble about his experiences. Pops has always had a great sense of humor." Nathan remembers asking his grandfather what was going through his mind before he took off from the carrier, expecting to hear something profound and exhilarating. "Well," replied Dick, "to tell you the truth—I was just trying not to mess up the preflight checklist because I was only a second lieutenant and I didn't want to get yelled at by the lieutenant colonel sitting right next to me." Nathan's brother Elliot graduated from West Point in 2015. He served in the army for two years, then transferred to the Air Force in 2017. He is currently serving as an E-8 Joint Surveillance Target Attack Radar System (JSTARS) crewmember.

The last Doolittle reunion was held in April 2013 at Ft. Walton Beach, Florida. Only three Raiders were able to attend—Dick Cole, Ed Saylor, and David Thatcher. The fourth surviving Raider, Bob Hite, was too ill to attend. They decided to have one last meeting to open the bottle of Hennessy cognac for the final toast, rather than wait for just the last two survivors, as originally planned. Accordingly, they met on November 9, 2013, at the Air Force Museum at Wright Patterson AFB to open the bottle and to have the final toast. Again, only Cole (age ninety-eight), Saylor (age ninety-four), and Thatcher (age ninety-two) were able to attend, since Hite (age ninety-three) was still too ill to travel. As the most senior of the survivors, Dick Cole opened the bottle of cognac—dated 1896, the year of Doolittle's birth. "Gentlemen, I propose a toast to those we lost on the mission and those who have passed away since," said Cole. "Thank you very much and may they rest in peace." Saylor and Thatcher sipped from their own goblets, and Hite watched from home via the Internet. Preceding the toast, acting air force secretary Eric Fanning and air force chief of staff Gen. Mark A. Welsh III spoke of the Raiders' courage and the significance of their mission to air force history.

Okerstrom's *Dick Cole's War* gives us a peek into Cole's droll sense of humor. Dick went to Kansas City in 2014 to appear in a program about the 1st Air Commandos. A member of the audience asked Dick what he thought about the final toast ceremony, where the last few surviving Raiders opened the 117-year-old cognac. He responded, "Well, it was good, but I thought they were kind of chintzy. I would have liked more." Another member of the audience asked him what was his most memorable moment about the Raid, and he responded, "When my parachute opened."

As of this writing, Dick is the only survivor of the Raid. He celebrated his 102nd birthday in September 2017. As the last of the Raiders, Dick has dedicated himself to continuing the legacy of the Raiders by raising money for the James H. Doolittle Scholarship Fund. In early 2017, Dick's son Rich sent this letter to his father: "When people meet me and find out that you are my dad, they are naturally impressed and assume that I am proud of you because of the Raid and your other exploits in World War II. They are correct. I am very proud of you for what you did in World War II; however, my pride stems from a much-deeper place. I remember always wanting to fly airplanes, like my dad. It wasn't until I was in the Air Force a few years that I began to understand the meaning of being in the military. It wasn't about being a fighter pilot and screaming around at the speed of heat (although that was a lot of fun). It was about being a military officer first and a pilot second. I came to realize that you volunteered to go to war not because you were a thrill seeker or wanted to make rank. You were defending our constitution against all enemies, foreign and domestic. You were doing exactly what you said you would do, regardless of the consequences. You swore an oath before God and it meant something to you. It meant everything to you. I know of no greater gift a father can give to his son; the willingness to give my life for my God, my country, and my family, like my dad. I count it as an honor, a privilege, and one of God's great Blessings in my life to have you as my father."

HENRY A. POTTER
Navigator

Pre-Raid

Hank was born on September 22, 1918, in Pierre, South Dakota. He graduated from high school in 1936 and started college at Yankton College in Yankton, South Dakota, in 1937. After two years, he transferred to the University of Oregon at Eugene. In the spring of 1940 while at the university, he witnessed an aerobatic display by a visiting army air corps team, and that sparked his interest in flying. In August 1940, he enlisted in the army air corps at Sturgis, Meade County, South Dakota. He was put on a train and sent to Primary Flying School at Oxnard, California. However, he washed out of pilot training, so immediately went to navigator school at Barksdale Field, Louisiana, graduating in 1941. Following navigator school, he was assigned to the 17th Bomb Group, McChord Field, Washington. Because of Pearl Harbor, he was assigned to fly patrol missions along the coast of Washington and Oregon to search for Japanese submarines. He did that until the group was transferred to Columbia, South Carolina, early in 1942. It was in Columbia that he had the opportunity to volunteer for a secret mission.

In *War Stories II: Heroism in the Pacific*, Oliver North quotes Potter's comments about volunteering for the Raid: "When we got to Columbia, South Carolina, Doolittle gathered the flight crews together in a hangar and briefed us, stating, 'We're gonna need volunteers for a dangerous mission that will be of great importance to the American war effort.' Nobody could figure out where he wanted us to go or what he wanted us to do when we got there, but if Jimmy Doolittle was going, we wanted to be there. He sent us to Eglin Field in Florida, where the pilots learned how to take off at short distances and the rest of us got the additional training in navigation, bombing, and firing machine guns. I don't think that any one of us had any lack of confidence that we'd be able to make it. After all, we were flying with the premier pilot in the Air Corps at that time. If he couldn't do it, it wasn't going to be done."

Post-Raid

Upon return from China in June 1942, Hank rejoined the 17th Bomb Group, which by then was flying B-26s—the Martin Marauder. In December, they went to North Africa to help drive the Germans out of Africa. When the Africa tour concluded, Hank returned to the States and was assigned to visit aircraft factories, oil refineries, and other defense-critical locations to tell the public about the war and to boost morale. He was next posted to the Office of the Air Force Inspector General. The remainder of the war was spent flying with and checking the training of B-17, B-24, and B-29 combat units and crews before they were sent overseas.

By the end of the war, Hank was based in the Washington, DC, area, where he met his future wife, Adell. She was a WAVE assigned to the US Navy Hydrographic Office and worked in the section that prepared aeronautical charts. They were married in November 1946 and had six children: Teresa, Karen, Cheryl, Cynthia, Monica, and Stephen. Following the war and until his retirement, Hank was assigned to various commands, such as the Air Proving Ground, Missile Test Center, Supreme Headquarters Allied Powers Europe (SHAPE), and Headquarters, US Air Force. Hank retired from the air force in 1970 as a colonel and settled in Austin, Texas, where he became active in the Confederate Air Force. After forty years of happy marriage, Adell died in December 1986. Hank died on May 27, 2002, at Seton Hospital in Austin at the age of eighty-three. He was buried in the Capitol Memorial Park in Pflugerville, Texas.

FRED ANTHONY BRAEMER
Bombardier

Pre-Raid
Fred was born on January 31, 1918, in Seattle, Washington. He graduated from Ballard High School in Seattle in 1935 and shortly thereafter enlisted in the army at Ft. Jay, New York. Fred served in the infantry and military intelligence until September 1938, when he left the service for a year. He enlisted in the army air corps in September 1939 and was trained as a bombardier. He was a staff sergeant at the time of the Raid.

Post-Raid
After the Raid, Fred remained in the China-Burma-India theater and flew twenty-six combat missions with the "Burma Bridge Busters" until July 1943, when he returned to the States. He became a bombardier instructor in July 1943 and was commissioned a second lieutenant in the US Army Air Force in January 1945. Late that same year, he was released from active duty and joined the Air Force Reserve. Lt. Braemer was recalled to active duty for the Korean War in September 1951. He flew twenty-eight combat missions as a B-29 bombardier until June 1953. After the war, Fred served as a navigator, bombardier, and aircraft observer on B-47 bombers until December 1957, when he reverted to enlisted status and was trained as an air traffic control operator. He served in Wheelus Air Base, Libya, and Whiteman AFB, Missouri. He regained his commission as captain in 1965 and was assigned to MacDill AFB, Florida. Fred's wife's name was Lucille. Fred retired from the air force in 1966, and he died of a heart attack while shoveling snow on February 2, 1989. He is buried in the Calvary Cemetery in Lincoln, Nebraska.

PAUL JOHN LEONARD
Flight Engineer/Gunner

Pre-Raid

Paul's tombstone says he was born on June 28, 1914, at Roswell, New Mexico, but other sources have erroneously quoted his birth date as June 19, 1912. He attended high school for two years before enlisting in the army at Ft. Bliss, Texas, on July 13, 1931. He received training as an airplane mechanic, and after assignments to units at Kelly Field, Texas; Chanute Field, Illinois; and Lowry Field, Colorado, he was assigned to the 37th Bomb Squadron in May 1941.

Post-Raid

Leonard earned the great respect of Jimmy Doolittle. After Doolittle and Leonard reunited after the bailout, they returned to the wreckage of their plane to see if there was anything useful they could salvage. When Doolittle saw the wreckage, he became terribly depressed and expressed the thought that he probably would be court-martialed for botching the Raid. However, Leonard disagreed heartily and stated his belief that Doolittle would be given a new plane and promoted to general. He told Doolittle that when the army did that, he would want to fly with Doolittle again as his crew chief. This brought tears to Doolittle's eyes, since this was the greatest compliment that a mechanic could give to a pilot. Doolittle accepted the offer and made good on it later. When Doolittle got back to Washington and was preparing to take command of the 4th Bomber Wing of the 8th Air Force, he arranged for T.Sgt. Leonard to be assigned as his crew chief.

Leonard remained in the China-Burma theater after the Raid until June 1942, when he returned to the States to become crew chief for Gen. Doolittle. M.Sgt. Leonard served in England and North Africa from September 1942 until January 5, 1943, when he was killed by enemy aircraft at Youks-les-Bains, Algeria. Leonard was still serving with Doolittle at the time. The day before, Doolittle had gone into town for a meeting with some ground commanders, leaving Leonard to take care of his plane. About midnight, the Germans came over and bombed the airfield. Doolittle couldn't return until the next morning. When he found the plane, he realized that Paul had moved it to the other side of the field and had used the top turret gun to shoot back at the German planes. Doolittle couldn't find Leonard but soon found a bomb crater nearby and deduced what had happened. After emptying the B-25's machine guns, Leonard had jumped into an earlier bomb crater for protection. Another bomb dropped on him, killing him instantly. All that was left for Doolittle to find was

Paul's left hand, with his wristwatch still in place. Doolittle had to write Paul's widow, Lois, and tell her the bad news. Doolittle said many years later that Paul's loss was his greatest personal tragedy of the war.

Leonard's remains initially were buried at Tebessa, Algeria, and were later reburied at the Santa Fe National Cemetery, Santa Fe, New Mexico.

Crew No. 2

```
Pilot.........................Lt. Travis Hoover
Copilot...................Lt. William N. Fitzhugh
Navigator....................Lt. Carl R. Wildner
Bombardier.................Lt. Richard E. Miller
Flight Engineer/Gunner....S.Sgt. Douglas V. Radney
```

TRAVIS HOOVER
Pilot

Pre-Raid

Travis was born on September 21, 1917, in Melrose, New Mexico. He spent most of his school years in Riverside, California, and graduated from Riverside Polytechnic High School in 1936. He earned an AA from Riverside Junior College in 1938, and a BA degree in international relations in 1949 from the University of California.

Travis enlisted in the California National Guard in November 1938 and entered flying cadet pilot training in the regular army in August 1939 at the Ryan School of Aeronautics in San Diego. He completed pilot training at Randolph and Kelly Fields and was commissioned a second lieutenant in May 1940. After duty at Barksdale Field and Lowey Field flying B-18s, he was assigned to Pendleton, Oregon, in 1941. He volunteered for a secret dangerous mission and in February 1942 was sent to Eglin AFB for special training in the B-25. The B-25 Mitchell was such a dramatic improvement over the depression-impoverished air corps' prior craft that the men of the 17th were thrilled to have them. Twenty-four-year-old Hoover was quoted in Craig Nelson's *The First Heroes* as saying, "The B-25 was a really superior airplane, right on the cutting edge of technology for medium bombardment." The first aerial combat experience for Lt. Hoover was on April 18, 1942, as the pilot of the second B-25 to fly from the carrier USS *Hornet*, making the first strike against the Japanese homeland of World War II.

Travis and his crew had trouble finding their designated target area. He is quoted in C. V. Glines's *The Doolittle Raid* as saying: "There was no good target in the exact area as indicated on the target map so we selected two factory buildings and storehouses. There was not sufficient time to climb to 1,500 feet, so we leveled off at 900 feet and Dick Miller, our bombardier, toggled off the bombs manually in succession at 215 mph. We then dove back down to the rooftops and followed a zigzag course along the west side of Tokyo and Yokohama." Travis caught sight of Doolittle's plane, so he followed him west toward the Chinese coast as the weather worsened. Visibility became terrible and night was approaching as they neared the coast. Travis tried to climb to fly over the mountains toward Chuhsien, but the left engine started cutting out. He immediately changed plans and started looking for a place to land along the coastline. He found a series of small rice paddies and made a wheels-up landing. The landing was a good one and nobody was injured. Hoover decided to burn the plane to deny any value to the Japanese, and he set fire to the engines with a gas-soaked tarpaulin. The crew took their equipment and rations and headed westward, not knowing if they were in Japanese-held territory. After a couple of days, they met a friendly farmer and learned they were in free China territory. They were soon met and taken into custody by about thirty Chinese guerrilla soldiers. They met up with other Raiders and eventually reached the safety of Chungking on May 14.

Post-Raid

After the Tokyo Raid and a promotion to captain, Hoover was brought back from China to Washington, DC, and assigned as commander of the newly formed 379th Bomb Squadron of the 310th Bomb Group. He flew the squadron across the North Atlantic and down to North Africa to fight against Rommel's German forces. Hoover served in aerial combat for two more years as squadron and group commander in North Africa and Italy, flying B-25 medium bombers and B-24 heavy bombers. When scheduled to return to the United States, he elected to remain overseas in combat, transferring to a P-38 fighter unit, the 82nd Fighter Group, thus becoming a dive bomber and fighter pilot. He flew a combined total of seventy-three combat missions in World War II, experiencing many terrifying close calls.

With promotion to colonel, Hoover had several interesting stateside assignments, such as instructor of air operations of the Command and General Staff School at Leavenworth, Kansas, where he met and later married Kay Snyder in December 1947. He also worked in top-secret war plans at the Pentagon. An interesting peacetime overseas assignment was as commander of the air base and American forces at Adana, Turkey, where he got to fly F-100 jet fighter bombers. Subsequently, he spent two years as commander of the Technical Training School at Keesler Air Base, Mississippi, from where he retired in October 1969 to grow citrus fruit in the Texas Rio Grande valley and to build apartments in San Antonio, Texas.

Col. Hoover and his wife, Kay, lived in San Antonio for twenty years prior to moving to Joplin, Missouri, in 1988. C. V. Glines informs us in *The First Heroes* that when Kay realized she had terminal cancer, she decided she wanted to spend her last days near her grandchildren in Joplin. Travis agreed, so he sold the house and they moved to Joplin, where Kay had about three good years with the grandkids before she died. He had one stepdaughter, Beverly, whose husband is Jim Zerkel, with five grandsons and six great-grandchildren. Kay died in 1990, and Travis died in Joplin on January 17, 2004, at the age of eighty-six. He was buried at Ft. Sam Houston National Cemetery in San Antonio, Texas.

WILLIAM N. FITZHUGH
Copilot

Pre-Raid
William N. Fitzhugh was born February 18, 1915, at Temple, Texas. He was a student at the University of Texas, where he graduated in 1938. He entered the aviation cadet program in November 1940 and completed it in July 1941, with a commission as second lieutenant. His first assignment was as a B-25 copilot with the 17th Bomb Group until he was selected for the Raid in February 1942.

Post-Raid
After the Doolittle Raid, Bill remained in China for eighteen months and was stationed at Kunming. He returned to the States and was in Memphis flying transport planes before being sent to Mobile as a test pilot at Brookley Field, Alabama. He served a total of five and a half years on active duty, being released from the air force in 1946, then spent three more years in the reserves.

While at Brookley Field, Bill met his future wife, Dorothea, on a blind date in May 1944. Dorothea was working as a draftsman on the base, and they were married in August 1944. Their first son, John Patterson Fitzhugh, was born in August 1945. After the air force, the family first moved to Galveston and then back to Mobile, where their second son, Michael Dean Fitzhugh, was born in January 1949. They named him Dean, after Dean Hallmark—one of the Raiders. Twelve years later, their third son, Mark Lee Fitzhugh, was born in April 1961.

Bill's first son, John, entered the navy OCS program with the help of "Hank" Miller, the naval officer who trained the Raiders on short takeoffs from carriers. John made a career of the navy, retiring as a full commander. His second son, Mike, was in the National Guard and had a career as a banker in Mobile. His third son, Mark, became an Episcopal priest and worked for the Alabama State Children's Rehabilitation Service in Birmingham.

Bill worked for an insurance company in Mobile for many years and died there on August 31, 1981. He was buried in the Mobile Memorial Gardens, Mobile, Alabama.

CARL R. WILDNER
Navigator

Pre-Raid
Carl Richard Wildner was born on May 18, 1915, in Holyoke, Massachusetts. He graduated from Amherst High School in 1932 and earned a BS in agriculture

from Massachusetts State College in 1937. He was commissioned in the Army Cavalry Reserve from ROTC in 1937. He entered the army's aviation cadet program in 1940 and graduated as a navigator and army air corps second lieutenant in June 1941. He was selected for the Raid in February 1942.

Post-Raid
Before leaving China, Carl received a Chinese medal from Madam Chiang Kai-Shek, which became part of a movie newsreel in American theaters. After the Doolittle Raid, Carl was assigned to duty in India, where he remained until July 1943. He returned to the States and served as a navigation instructor at various bases. In 1946, he was assigned to Alaska and subsequently served in Newfoundland and Germany until discharged from active duty in November 1954. After active duty, he worked as a supply cataloguer for the US Marine Corps and he retired from the Air Force Reserve in 1962 as a lieutenant colonel.

Carl had two children with his first wife. Son Charles Wildner was born in 1949 and he had a career as a software developer. Daughter Wini Wildner Knowlton was a CPA and Mary Kay team manager. Carl married his second wife, Hilda, in Philadelphia in 1958. He died on March 7, 1994, and is buried in the Indiantown Gap National Cemetery in Annville, Pennsylvania.

RICHARD E. MILLER
Bombardier

Pre-Raid
Richard Ewing Miller was born on March 2, 1916, in Ft. Wayne, Indiana. He had two years of college and then enlisted as a flying cadet in February 1939 at Ft. Benjamin Harrison, Indiana. He was eliminated from pilot training in April 1939 but reenlisted as a flying cadet for bombardier training in May 1941. He received his bombardier rating and was commissioned a second lieutenant in December 1941.

Post-Raid
In *The Doolittle Raid* by C. V. Glines, Dick describes their encounter with the Chinese guerrillas this way: "About an hour after leaving the farmer we ran into a group of armed guerrillas who immediately robbed us of everything except our clothes. They took us into a small village. On the trip, another group of guerrillas fired at us from the hills by mistake. At the guerrilla headquarters, we were able to make them understand who we were by sign language, pictures, and some English, which they understood. They returned just about all our personal equipment except our pistols, which they promised to return later."

After the Doolittle Raid, Dick was assigned to the 319th Bomb Group and served in North Africa. He also served with the 37th Squadron of the 17th Bomb Group. Dick was killed in action on a bombing mission over North Africa on January 22, 1943—less than a year after the Raid. He is buried in the Lindenwood Cemetery in Ft. Wayne, Indiana. The Richard E. Miller Center at Grissom Air Reserve Base, Bunker Hill, Indiana, was named after Dick to honor his service.

DOUGLAS VERNON RADNEY
Flight Engineer/Gunner

Pre-Raid

Douglas V. Radney was born on March 17, 1917, in Minneola, Texas. He graduated from Mexia High School in Mexia, Texas, in 1935 and entered the army in January 1936 at Ft. Bliss, Texas. He completed the aircraft mechanics school. While stationed at Scott Field, Belleville, Illinois, he met his future wife—Mary Jane—and they became engaged shortly after the Pearl Harbor attack. As Doug was training for the Doolittle Raid, he always told Mary Jane that he would let her know when he was going overseas, although security regulations prohibited them from discussing it. When Doug reached California a few days before his departure on the USS *Hornet*, he sent a letter to Mary in Kansas. At the end of the letter, he quoted a verse from Tennyson's famous poem *Crossing the Bar*, which said:

> "Sunset and evening star, and one clear call to me!
> May there be no mourning at the bar,
> when I put out to sea."

Mary knew instantly that this meant Doug was about to depart on his journey. Doug decided at the last moment that he wanted to send his fiancée an engagement ring, but all the crew members had been confined to quarters for security reasons. Doug discussed his problem with S.Sgt. Paul Leonard, who was serving as Jimmy Doolittle's aide, and also as flight engineer/gunner on Doolittle's B-25. Paul was going to town on business, so he volunteered to pick out a ring for Doug, and he mailed it to Mary in Kansas. After the Raid on April 18, 1942, it was four agonizing months before Mary received word that Doug was safe and had been seen by Paul Leonard in Allahabad, India, several days after the Raid.

In spite of being a superior medium bomber in most respects, the B-25Bs of this era were woefully inadequate in their armament, and they had some serious deficiencies in the reliability of the gun turrets. The turret power mechanism failed repeatedly so that the gunners could not rotate them to aim at enemy fighters boring in. Because of this, gunnery practice with the .50-caliber machine guns was delayed. Radney was quoted in C. V. Glines's *The Doolittle Raid* as saying this about the lack of experience with the guns: "I suppose I should have been concerned at the time but I don't remember being worried about anything much in those days. I knew that if the Boss thought things were OK, then we'd come out of it all right."

Post-Raid

After the Raid, Doug remained in the China-Burma-India theater, serving in the 11th Bomb Squadron under the leadership of Gen. Claire Chennault. While still serving as an engineer/gunner, he flew twenty-five missions and was credited with shooting down eight enemy aircraft. He returned to the States either in 1942 or 1943, and he married Mary Jane on July 7, 1943, in Greenville, South Carolina. Doug continued his career in the air force, was commissioned an officer in 1945, and completed pilot training. He attended the Aircraft Maintenance Officer School and spent the rest of his career as a pilot and an aircraft maintenance officer.

Doug served at many different bases, including Greenville Army Base, Maxwell Field, Craig Field, Lakeland AFB, Spence Field, Turner Field, Brooks Field, Tinker AFB, Eglin AFB, Mitchell AFB, and Richards-Gebaur AFB. He served overseas in Alaska as a cold-weather test pilot and maintenance officer and retired in May 1959 as a senior pilot after about twenty-three years of service at the rank of major.

Doug and Mary had three children: Douglas Vernon Radney II (born in 1945), Pamela Jane Radney (1948), and J. Randolph Radney (1954). Doug Jr. made a career in the air force, retiring as a master sergeant, after which he worked as a software engineer for Lockheed-Martin. Pamela Jayne became a wildlife researcher for the US Forestry Service, and Randolph became an associate professor of linguistics and sessional professor of philosophy at Trinity Western University at Langley, British Columbia, Canada.

After retiring from the air force, Doug flew for a small corporation, and his wife frequently served as his copilot. Doug died on January 28, 1994, and was buried at Ft. Logan National Cemetery, Denver, Colorado.

Lt. Charles Ozuk Jr., Lt. Robert Gray, Sgt. Aden Jones, Lt. Jacob "Shorty" Manch, Cpl. Leland Faktor

Crew No. 3

Pilot..........................Lt. Robert M. Gray

Copilot........................Lt. Jacob E. Manch

Navigator..................Lt. Charles J. Ozuk Jr.

Bombardier.....................Sgt. Aden E. Jones

Flight Engineer/Gunner.......Cpl. Leland D. Faktor

ROBERT MANNING GRAY
Pilot

Pre-Raid

Bob Gray was born on May 24, 1919, at Elijah, Texas. The family moved to Killeen, Texas, shortly thereafter, where Bob's father bought a hardware store and plumbing business. Bob graduated from Killeen High School and attended Texas A&M College and John Tarleton College. Bob majored in aeronautical engineering and was in the class of 1940. From Tarleton, he entered the army air corps in June 1940 and became a flying cadet. He completed his training at Randolph and Kelly Fields in February 1941 and then was stationed at various fields on the West Coast. He served as a B-25 pilot with the 17th Bomb Group at McChord Field, Washington, from February 1941 until he was selected for the Raid in February 1942. His B-25 in the Raid was named the "*Whiskey Pete*."

"Shorty" Manch reported in C. V. Glines's *The Doolittle Raid* that Gray held a meeting with his crew on their way to Japan. "Bob took a vote among the crew that if we were badly damaged by gunfire, what we wanted to do. All the members of the crew with the exception of Gray stated that if they had the chance, they would like to bail out. Bob said that if he had the chance, he would let us out, then he was going to pick out the biggest building in Tokyo and stick "*Whisky Pete*" right in the middle of it."

Post-Raid

Bob and his crew successfully escaped through China, but Bob didn't get a chance to return home. He was assigned to the China-Burma-India theater, where he was promoted to captain and flew with the famous Flying Tigers. On October 18, 1942, while flying in heavy fog over the Burmese mountains known as "the Hump," his plane's engines failed. Bob was killed at the age of twenty-three as he and his crew crashed on a high mountain. He died just six months to the day after the famous raid on Japan. He was initially buried at Barrackpore, India, but nine years later was reburied in Killeen, Texas, with full military honors. The Killeen Army Air Base was renamed the Robert Gray Army Airfield in his honor.

JACOB EARL MANCH
Copilot

Pre-Raid

"Shorty" Manch was born on December 26, 1918, in Staunton, Virginia. He attended Hampden Sydney College and Washington & Lee College (both in

Virginia), and Southern Methodist University in Texas, majoring in business administration. He was appointed a second lieutenant in the Infantry Reserve in May 1940, and then he enlisted as a flying cadet in February 1941. He graduated from advanced flying school at Stockton Field, California, in September 1941. He was assigned to the 17th Bomb Group, 95th Squadron, Pendleton, Oregon, in October 1941, from which he was selected for Doolittle's team.

Post-Raid

After the Raid, Manch bailed out of his B-25 over China, and he successfully escaped the pursuing Japanese. After safely reaching the ground with his parachute jump, Shorty started walking the next morning. His height caused him some surprising problems, according to C. V. Glines's account in his book *The Doolittle Raid* (some books report his height as 6′4″; another book, at 6′6″; others, at 6′7″). Shorty came upon a Chinese man and woman who took one look at this giant and fled terrified into the woods. Most Chinese peasants had never seen a white man before, and certainly not a man of such height. He then came upon an old woman gathering firewood. "The sight of me threw her into a panic," Manch said. "She threw her sticks down and hobbled off on her wrapped feet." Manch plodded on until he was dead tired and hungry; he sat down in a creek with water up to his waist and wondered what to do next. He eventually found some friendly Chinese who took him to the safety of their village.

Shorty was retained in China and assigned to aerial combat duties for a little over a year with the China Air Task Force, where he flew with the aircraft ferry command in the India-China area. In July 1943, Shorty was sent back to the States and was assigned as commanding officer at Hill Field, Ogden, Utah, where he was a test pilot on planes sent back from combat to be checked.

After attending the Command and Staff School at Leavenworth, Kansas, in 1945 and the Counter Intelligence Corps School at Hollibird Signal Depot in 1947, he was assigned as chief of intelligence and inspector general at Watson Laboratories (part of the Air Material Command). In 1950, Manch was transferred to Korea as air liaison officer with the 7th Infantry Division, and he later served with the 452nd Bomber Wing at Pusan, Korea. He was serving in Korea when the Chinese invaded, and he fought in the Chosin Reservoir conflict. In 1951, he transferred to the 35th Fighter Wing at Johnson Air Base, Japan.

In 1953, Manch was transferred to Nellis AFB in Las Vegas, where he served as base operations officer from 1953 until 1956, when he became the base inspector at Nellis. On March 24, 1958, Lt. Col. Manch was killed in a training flight near Las Vegas. He was flying a T-33 jet trainer when the engine flamed out. Shorty got his passenger to bail out safely, while he stayed with the plane to guide it away from populated areas. He bailed out at the last minute, but he was too low for his parachute to deploy properly. He was buried at Arlington National Cemetery, Arlington, Virginia. The Jacob E. Manch Elementary School was named in his honor in Las Vegas. Manch was married to Dollie Lee Mathis, and they had no children. Lee Manch died in October 2003.

CHARLES JOHN OZUK JR.
Navigator

Pre-Raid

Charles was born June 13, 1916, at Vesta Heights, Pennsylvania. He graduated from Carl Schurz High School and enlisted in the army air corps on November 9, 1939, at Chanute Field, Illinois. Charles attended radio and mechanics school at Chanute Field before entering pilot training in early 1940. He was eliminated from pilot training but reenlisted for navigator training in late 1940. He graduated with the rating of navigator and was commissioned a second lieutenant at McChord Field, Washington, in June 1941. His first assignment was as a B-25 Mitchell navigator with the 95th Bomb Squadron at McChord Field, Washington, from February 1941 until he was selected for the Doolittle mission in February 1942.

Post-Raid

Charles bailed out of his B-25 but landed on the side of a cliff and sustained a severe leg injury. He hung suspended in the harness of his parachute for twenty-four hours before being rescued by the Chinese.

Following the Raid, Charles was kept in China and served in the China-Burma-India theater until July 1942. Back in the States, he attended B-26 navigational training at Lakeland, Florida, and Ft. Wayne, Indiana. Upon completion of training, he was deployed with the 441st Bomb Squadron to North Africa in December 1942. Capt. Ozuk served as a B-26 navigator until November 1943, when he was injured in a crash landing on his twenty-seventh combat mission. After recovering from his injuries, he returned to his squadron in January 1944 and flew another twelve combat missions before being injured in another crash landing in March 1944. He was returned to the States in May 1944 and served as a navigator instructor until he was medically discharged in April 1945.

After the war, Ozuk worked as an electronics engineer for Motorola in Chicago when the television industry was booming. After retirement, Charles and his wife, Georgian, lived in Mundelein, Illinois, and then San Antonio, Texas. Capt. Ozuk died at age ninety-four on October 9, 2010, in San Antonio and was buried in the St. Louis Cemetery in Castroville, Texas.

ADEN EARL JONES
Bombardier

Pre-Raid
Aden was born on September 7, 1920, at Flint, Michigan, and his family soon moved to Pasadena, California, in 1923. He attended Jefferson Elementary and Washington Junior High and graduated from Pasadena Junior College, West Campus, where he majored in mechanics. After college, Aden first tried to enlist in the naval aviation corps, but he was rejected as being too tall at 6´4˝; he was four inches over the navy's limit. Undaunted, he then enlisted in the army air corps in September 1939 and trained at March Field, Pendleton Field, and Eglin Field before going on the Raid.

Post-Raid
Jones was the first crew member to bail out of his B-25 over China. He exited through the lower door and only had three swings of his chute before he landed hard in rocks and shrubs on a mountaintop. He spent the first night alone in the rain, wrapped in his parachute. He had quite a struggle to survive, going without food for three days, until he reached a Chinese village, where guides fed him and conducted him on a long trek back to civilization.

Before returning to the States, Sgt. Jones went on duty with the 11th Bomber Squadron in Burma for sixteen months, where he flew seventy-nine combat missions. They flew out of small hidden airfields carved out of the jungle in India and would bomb occupied Burma and land in unoccupied China. Then they would reverse the procedure.

Back in the States, Aden served as a flight instructor in Louisiana until he was discharged in October 1945. He served another tour of duty from May 1947 to December 1948, leaving the service as a lieutenant. He met and married Doris Nettie Vick in 1952, and they adopted a son, Raymond Earl Jones, in 1955. Aden soon went to work for Lockheed Aircraft in Ontario, California, where he worked for thirty-two years—most of it as a flight electrical-instrument checkout mechanic.

Aden died on March 9, 1983, and was buried at Forest Lawn Memorial Park, Covina, California.

LELAND DALE FAKTOR
Flight Engineer/Gunner

Pre-Raid

Leland was born on May 17, 1921, on a farm one mile west of Plymouth, Iowa. He graduated from high school in 1940. Pursuing a long-held passion for flying, he enlisted in the army air corps in August 1940 with the intention of becoming a pilot. He was attending the airplane mechanics school at Chanute Field in Illinois when Pearl Harbor was attacked. His first assignment was with the 95th Bomb Squadron at McChord Field, Washington, where he was selected for the Raid in February 1942. In his last letter home to his mother from Eglin Field, Florida, he explained that it was a secret mission, and that he couldn't tell her where he was going. He said he would be a hero or in heaven the next time they heard about him or from him.

Post-Raid

Cpl. Leland died at the age of twenty on the day of the Raid, when he tried to bail out of his fuel-empty B-25. His body was found near a partially opened parachute the following morning. The American government got temporary permission to bury Cpl. Faktor on Chinese soil, so one month after his death, he was buried with full military honors near the village of Wang Tsun (maybe Wan Tseun), 450 miles southwest of Shanghai. David Thatcher, another Raider, attended the funeral, which was conducted by John Birch—a US military intelligence officer and Baptist minister (this John Birch was killed in 1945 by armed supporters of the Communist Party of China, and the John Birch Society was named after him). The grave was disguised as a typical Chinese grave, so the Japanese wouldn't know an American was buried there. In 1949, the Chinese government suggested it was time to remove Leland's remains. The family had a choice to rebury him in Hawaii or back on the mainland. His parents decided to have him back in Plymouth. Seven years after his death, Leland was reburied in the Bohemian Cemetery, Plymouth, Iowa. He was the last Raider to return from China.

In May 1978, a dormitory building at Chanute Field was named Faktor Hall in his honor, with eighty-one-year-old Gen. Doolittle as the honored guest.

Crew No. 4

Pilot......................Lt. Everett W. Holstrom

Copilot...................Lt. Lucian N. Youngblood

Navigator....................Lt. Harry C. McCool

Bombardier................Sgt. Robert J. Stephens

Flight Engineer/Gunner........Cpl. Bert M. Jordan

EVERETT WAYNE HOLSTROM
Pilot

Pre-Raid

Everett Holstrom was born on May 4, 1916, at Cottage Grove, Oregon. He graduated from Pleasant Hill High School, Pleasant Hill, Oregon, in 1934 and attended Oregon State University as a forestry major until entering military service at Ft. Lewis, Washington, in December 1939. He was commissioned a second lieutenant and rated a pilot upon graduation from Randolph Field in 1940. Because of his red hair, he picked up the nickname "Brick." Brick had the unique experience of sinking the first Japanese submarine off the West Coast on December 25, 1941, while a member of the 95th Bomb Squadron.

Post-Raid

Brick and his crew bailed out over China after the Raid. He landed in a large bush in complete darkness, struggling for a while to get free before giving up and pulling the parachute around him for a few hours of sleep. When dawn came, he was glad that he hadn't struggled free the night before, since he was on the edge of a 50-foot drop onto rocks. For the next six nights, Brick hiked through Japanese-occupied territory; he had bailed out just south of Hanchow Bay. There is some contradictory information about how Brick got to the safety of Chunking. One report said that a band of guerillas smuggled him by bus to the airport at Hengyang, where a US Air Corps C-47 picked him up and flew him to India. However, Craig Nelson's book *The First Heroes* (p. 199) states that Holstrom and Youngblood joined up with McCool and Jordan and that a group of Chinese soldiers took them by truck to meet up with a train that took them to Chunking. A third report was found in C. V. Glines's book *The Doolittle Raid*, in which Glines says about Holstrom and Davey Jones that "the group travelled to Hengyang on May 3rd and were taken by DC-3 to Chungking on May 14" (p. 89).

Brick remained in the China-Burma-India theater for fourteen months after the Raid, flying B-25s out of Kunming under Gen. Claire Chennault. He assumed command of the 11th Bomb Squadron from mid-1942 until the end of 1943. Following World War II, Brick was assigned to the SAC (Strategic Air Command) headquarters as an operations staff officer. From 1950 to 1953 he was a member of the 91st Bomb Wing as director of operations and also as deputy wing commander. He moved with the wing from Barksdale AFB, Louisiana, to Lockbourne AFB, Ohio. From 1953 to 1955, Holstrom was assigned to Second Air Force Headquarters as director of operations. For the next two years, he commanded the 301st Bomb Wing at Barksdale AFB then returned to SAC headquarters from 1957 to 1959 as chief of the Operations

Plans Division. On September 4, 1959, he assumed duties as commander of the Second Air Force's 4130th Strategic Wing, Bergstrom AFB, Texas. He assumed command of the 43rd Bomb Wing, SAC's first bombardment wing in June 1961, and was promoted to brigadier general on March 1, 1964, making him just one of five men on the Raid who achieved the officer rank of general.

Brick and Hattie had a large family of five children: Susan (born in 1942), Wayne (1944), Marianne (1945), John (1947), and David (1949). They lived all over the United States in such places as New York, California, South Dakota, Alaska, Louisiana, Nebraska, and Arizona. His last tour of duty took them to SHAPE (Supreme Headquarters Allied Powers Europe—the central command of NATO military forces) in Paris and Belgium. Brick retired in 1969 after thirty years of service, with twenty years in SAC, flying B-29s, B-45s, B-47s, B-52s, B-58s, and U-2s. In Craig Nelson's *The First Heroes*, Brick is quoted as saying, "After the war, I continued on in the service for a total of thirty years, and my proudest moment besides the raid was getting the Convair B-58, our first supersonic bomb wing, combat ready in the SAC inventory. In retirement, my wife Hattie and I were lucky to have enough assets to do a lot of travelling. We went back to Europe about fifteen times and travelled over South America and the Far East, including China. I think the 'been there, done that' thing pretty well describes us."

Upon retirement, Brick and Hattie bought a new car in New Jersey and set out to drive cross-country. In Monterey County, they met the owners of Carmel Valley Manor, a residential retirement facility. The Holstroms fell in love with the area, and the owners of Carmel Valley Manor offered Brick the job of manager. He gladly accepted the offer and served for thirteen years until his second retirement in 1983.

Gen. Holstrom died of a brain hemorrhage at age eighty-four at the Carmel Valley Manor's medical unit on December 2, 2000. He was buried at Arlington National Cemetery, Arlington, Virginia.

LUCIAN NEVELSON YOUNGBLOOD
Copilot

Pre-Raid
Lucian was born on May 26, 1918, at Pampa, Texas. Shortly thereafter, the family moved to Waco, Texas. He played tackle for the Waco High School Tigers and played guard for the basketball team. After graduating from Waco High School in 1936, he joined the Texas National Guard and served with the 143rd Infantry until enlisting in the US Army in September 1936. He served with Company I of the 23rd Infantry at Ft. Sam Houston until his discharge in

August 1938. He then attended college for two years at St. Mary's University in San Antonio, until his enlistment in the aviation cadet program of the army air corps in November 1940. He was commissioned a second lieutenant and awarded his pilot wings in July 1941.

In October 1941, Lucian married L'Gean Manning of Waco, Texas. His friends from the 95th Bombardment Squadron held their sabers to form an arch for the bride and bridegroom to walk under as they left the church. They never had any children. Lt. Youngblood's first assignment was as a B-25 Mitchell pilot with the 95th Bomb Squadron of the 17th Bomb Group at Pendleton Army Airfield, Oregon, where he was selected for the Doolittle mission. Youngblood's plane in the Raid was named "Sea Hag."

Post-Raid

As soon as the "Sea Hag" dropped her bombs on the assigned targets, pilot Maj. Everett Holstrom turned and flew down the Japanese coast toward the China Sea. Lucian later reported in a Waco newspaper interview that "We hadn't been scratched by anti-aircraft or Zero fire, but as soon as we were over the China Sea, we began to suspect our fuel would run out and we would have to crash-land on the water. We got out our rubber raft, but a tailwind practically blew us to China and we were fifteen minutes beyond the coast before our tanks went dry."

Lucian and his crew safely bailed out over China at a point near and southeast of Shangjac. He wrote a manuscript a few years later, describing his escape through China. Various sympathetic Chinese helped him along the way. He finally met up with other members of the Raid in Chu Chien on April 25—seven days after the mission. Like many other Raiders, Lucian was assigned to the China-Burma-India theater after the Raid. He was assigned to the 11th Bombardment Squadron to fly B-25s, and he flew over twenty-five combat missions with that squadron. In July 1942, he was awarded the Silver Star for carrying out a low-level bombing raid on Nan Chang, China, in the face of intense antiaircraft fire and harassment by six Japanese fighters. Six Japanese airplanes were destroyed on the ground, along with several runways and various ground installations. In May 1943, Lucian returned to the States and was assigned to bases in South Carolina, New York, and Kansas for the remainder of World War II. He was assigned to Newfoundland from February 1946 until August 1948.

Maj. Youngblood was killed in an aircraft accident in the Serranias Delburro Mountains of Mexico on February 28, 1949. He was serving as executive officer of the 2150th Rescue Unit at Hamilton AFB, just north of San Francisco, and was flying in a C-47 transport on a routine flight from Hamilton Field to San Antonio. It took a large air search to locate the crash site. Lucian's death certificate said that he died from extensive cranial damage and severe third-degree burns. He was buried at Forest Park Lawndale Cemetery in Houston, Texas, and was inducted into the Texas Aviation Hall of Fame at Galveston. His wife, L'Gean, died in 2009 at age eighty-seven, and she had made a point of attending all the Raider reunions to honor Lucian and the Raiders. She was buried in the same plot with Lucian in Houston.

HARRY CLAYTON MCCOOL
Navigator

Pre-Raid
Harry was born on April 19, 1918, in La Junta, Colorado, and graduated from Beaver High School in Beaver, Oklahoma. He joined the Oklahoma National Guard in October 1936 and served in the artillery before receiving an honorable discharge in February 1940. He met his future wife, LaVerne, while attending the Institute of Technology in Weatherford, Oklahoma (now the Southwestern Oklahoma State University), where he earned a BS in science and mathematics. He joined the aviation cadet program and was awarded his navigator wings and commissioned a second lieutenant in June 1941. His first assignment was as a B-25 navigator with the 95th Bomb Squadron at Pendleton Field, Oregon, where he served until selected for the Raid in February 1942.

Post-Raid
When he and his crew members bailed out over China, Lt. McCool landed in the darkness on a mountaintop on his twenty-fourth birthday. He tied himself to a tree to avoid falling down the cliffs in the dark. It took him three days to get far enough down the mountain to find a woodcutter's hut. He tried to start a fire with an old straw mattress to dry out his wet clothes, but so many fleas jumped out of the fire pit that he had to go out in the rain again to find comfort and security from the parasites. Eventually, he joined the rest of his companions at Chunking. After a trip to India, McCool was attached to a flying unit at Calcutta.

On his thirteenth mission, Harry almost met his death due to an unusual incident. The pilot of his plane was a Texas boy called "Singing Boy Johnson." It was Johnson's last required mission, and he had never fired a shot at the enemy. He took the plane down and fired at a Japanese ship, and as they went around for a second shot, they were attacked. The bombardier was killed and one engine was gone, and they got 50 miles off the Japanese-held territory before ditching in the ocean off Burma. Working fast, Harry later reported, they grabbed two rubber life rafts and found that one had a malfunctioning inflator. "We were six men, one dead man, with the aircraft sinking and boats for only half of us," Harry remembered. "Somehow, both boats got inflated, tied together, and we climbed in and started drifting." They drifted to Oyster Island, an abandoned lighthouse, and stayed there two or three days with no food but plenty of water. Fearful of discovery and worried about food, they put water in cans and put out to sea with a makeshift sail held between their knees. For six days, the tide took them in and out while the current took them north. On the sixth night a typhoon wind from the south whipped them onto shore. They slept on the beach, and when they awakened, at least twenty-five Burmese were watching them. McCool said: "Three stayed on the beach, and three of us went into the brush and rice paddy area where we met a troop of Ghurkas who took us all back to a British group. They doctored our wounds and notified Calcutta we were safe. Our commanding officer flew a DC-2 down, landed on the sandy beach, and welcomed us aboard with a quart of Scotch. I had lost twenty pounds, and the others were generally weakened. After only a two-hour flight back, the air force had six roaring drunks deplaning."

In August 1942, McCool returned to a hero's welcome in Oklahoma City. Harry and LaVerne had three children: Patricia Ann (born in 1940), Peggy Sue (1942), and James Stanley (1948). After the war, McCool continued his military career and flew sixty-five missions in Europe. He was assigned to the 9th Air Force in England as navigator on B-26 bombers, planning and participating in many D-day missions over France and Germany, which he counted as his greatest contributions to the war effort. He earned an MS degree in systems management from the University of Southern California in 1959 and became deputy director for the Strategic Air Command. He had one tour of duty with the CIA in the 1950s. Harry had numerous intelligence assignments in such locations as French Morocco; Offutt AFB; Ft. Myer, Virginia; Andrews AFB; and the Pentagon. He retired from active duty as a lieutenant colonel from the Pentagon in 1966, and within one month he was working at Pearl Harbor as a civilian specialist on computer systems for the Pacific Fleet (CINCPACFLT). He worked there for twenty-two more years. Upon his second retirement around 1989, the McCools retired to the Air Force Villages in San Antonio, Texas. In *The First Heroes*, Craig Nelson quotes Harry as saying, "We lived near a number of other Tokyo Raiders. As career officers, we didn't have any roots. No one wanted, really, to go back to their childhood home. You come here and you're taken care of—if you want to go on a trip, you lock the front door and put a hold on your mail at the front desk, and take off. And then, San Antonio is an air force town, with four or five golf courses, three or four clubs, and four or five bases, terrific medical care. It's a fine place for a retired military man to live." Harry told his children never to visit them between the months of May and October, because he didn't want his neighbors to think they'd raised stupid kids who'd go to that hot and humid locale during those months. So the McCools would usually spend one of those summer months visiting the cool Colorado mountains.

LaVerne died in 2001 of Alzheimer's, and her cremains were scattered in the Colorado mountains. Harry died in San Antonio of prostate cancer on February 1, 2003, at the age of eighty-four. Harry wanted his ashes distributed where they would "flow to the ocean," so he was distributed to several family members who scattered his remains in the Atlantic, the Pacific, the Gulf of Mexico, the Missouri River, the Mississippi River, and some Colorado mountain lakes, as well as in each family's garden.

ROBERT JAMES STEPHENS
Bombardier

Pre-Raid
Robert was born on February 28, 1915, at Hobart, Oklahoma. At age five, he was orphaned when both his parents were killed in a tornado. He was raised by his grandmother—Mrs. Nannie Shelton—of Hobart, Oklahoma. He graduated from Hobart High School and entered military service as a private in November 1939 at Ft. Riley, Kansas. He completed bombardier school in June 1940, and mechanics school in February 1941. His first assignment was as a B-25 bombardier with the 95th Bomb Squadron at McChord Field, Washington, and then Pendleton Airfield, Oregon, where he was selected for the Raid in February 1942.

Post-Raid
Robert remained in China after the Raid—continuing to serve as a bombardier in the China-India-Burma theater until July 1943. After returning to the States, he was commissioned as a flight officer on February 11, 1944, with a rating as an aircraft observer. He retired with a physical disability on December 1, 1944. Robert died on April 13, 1959, and was buried at Rose Cemetery, Hobart, Oklahoma.

BERT M. JORDAN
Flight Engineer/Gunner

Pre-Raid
Bert was born on September 3, 1919, at Covington, Oklahoma. He entered military service in November 1939. He had basic training at Randolph Field, Texas, then attended aircraft maintenance school in Oakland, California. His

first assignment was as a B-25 mechanic and flight engineer with the 95th Bomb Squadron at Pendleton Airfield from January 1942 until he was selected for the Raid in February 1942.

Post-Raid

Someone asked Bert what was the most prominent memory of the Raid, and he answered, "Bailing out of the B-25 was the scariest part of the mission over Japan. You wondered where you were because it was raining so hard. Then the pilot says, 'It's time to go' via the intercom, and I reply, 'It's been a fine ride—I'll see you later,' and out I go. As soon as I'm out of the plane, I pulled the ripcord and the chute opened. 'What a relief!' I soon hear the sound of water hitting rocks, and about that time I hit the cold water. Bobbing up and down like a cork, I realized my chute was caught in the trees. I decided I had to cut myself loose, and lucky for me, I cut all the shrouds except one. That one swung me over to shallow water, where it was safe to cut the last shroud. Once high and dry, I stayed there the rest of that night and the next morning started walking downstream. Around midday, I came across eight Chinese and a scuffle broke out—they took my weapon and led me to a large village. I was taken to a building that surprisingly had a telephone. The Chinese made a call and handed me the phone; the voice on the other end spoke good English and said that he knew of the Japan Raid and that he would be there in the morning to take me out. The next morning, we left for another village, where I was reunited with two of my crew members. Another relief. The remaining trip out of China took approximately seven days and was very exhausting."

After the Raid, Bert continued to serve in the China-Burma-India theater, serving as a B-25 flight engineer and gunner with the 11th Bomb Squadron until October 1943, when he returned to the States. Back in the States, Bert met Lula "Judy" Smith, and they were married on December 4, 1943, in Charleston, Missouri. They had three children, all born in Enid, Oklahoma: Sherry Lee (born in 1945), Jay Loren (1946), and Judy Lynn (1954).

Bert had many assignments in aircraft maintenance, serving at stateside bases in Arizona, Florida, Kansas, New Mexico, Oklahoma, and Texas. He also served overseas in England, Germany, Guam, and Thailand. He retired from the air force as a chief master sergeant in July 1971, after thirty-two years of service and sixty-three missions. Bert died on April 3, 2001, just two months after his wife, Judy, passed away. He was buried in Georgetown Cemetery in Pottsboro, Texas.

Crew No. 5

Pilot.....................Capt. David M. Jones
Copilot....................Lt. Rodney R. Wilder
Navigator...................Lt. Eugene F. McGurl
Bombardier.................Lt. Denver V. Truelove
Flight Engineer/Gunner.......Sgt. Joseph W. Manske

DAVID MUDGETT JONES
Pilot

Pre-Raid

David "Davey" Jones was born December 18, 1913, at Marshfield, Oregon. He graduated from Tucson High School in Tucson, Arizona in 1932 then attended the University of Arizona in Tucson from 1932 to 1936. He enlisted in the Arizona National Guard and served one year in the cavalry prior to entering pilot training in 1937. After being commissioned a second lieutenant and gaining his pilot rating in June 1937, he was assigned to the 17th Bomb Group at March and McChord Fields.

In June 1939, David married Anita Maddox of Winters, Texas. They had three children: Jere Jean, who married Dennis Yeager of Ft. Worth, an attorney; David Jr., who married Jane Gibbs; and James, who married and divorced.

In early 1942, Jones volunteered for the Doolittle mission.

Post-Raid

Capt. Jones and his crew took off safely from the *Hornet* despite a leak in the bomb bay gas tank and proceeded for Tokyo. His bombs scored direct hits on a power station, oil tanks, and a large manufacturing plant. Continuing on to China, he flew on instruments in stormy weather until he estimated he was in the vicinity of Chuchow. His entire crew bailed out without injury and were the first to reach Chuchow, since they landed near and just southeast of it. After escaping from China, Capt. Jones returned to the States and was assigned as commander of the 319th Bomb Group in North Africa in September 1942. Only three months later, he was shot down over Bizerte, North Africa, and spent the next two and a half years as a prisoner of war in Stalag Luft III in Germany. On Finn John's website *Offbeat Oregon*, Finn summarizes Davey's prisoner experience: "Jones quickly developed a reputation in his prison camp for defiance and harassment of his German captors. Soon he was on the camp's 'X Committee,' or escape committee—the secret group of prisoners who controlled and coordinated all attempts to escape. After the war, Stalag Luft III and its X Committee became famous for the audacious bustout told of in the Steve McQueen movie *The Great Escape*. Jones led the digging team for the 'Harry' tunnel (the committee's plan involved three tunnels, named 'Tom', 'Dick', and 'Harry'; only 'Harry' made it to completion). In fact, the character of Capt. Virgil Hilts, played by Steve McQueen himself, was partly based on Jones."

Following the war, Davey had a short assignment in the War Plans Department of the Tactical Air Command, then assumed command of the 47th Bomb Wing in June 1952, at Langley AFB, Virginia, and then moved the wing to RAF Station, Sculthorpe, England. Upon returning to the States in

1955, he had these assignments: deputy chief of staff, operations, Air Proving Ground Command, Eglin AFB, Florida; director of the Joint ARDC / SAC B-58 Test Force at Carswell AFB, 1958; vice commander, Air Division, Wright Patterson AFB, 1961; program manager for the GAM-87 "Skybolt," 1961; deputy chief of staff / systems, at headquarters of Air Force Systems Command, Andrews AFB, Maryland, 1964; deputy associate administrator for Manned Space Flights, NASA, 1964; commander of the air force's Eastern Test Range, Patrick AFB, Florida, 1967.

He also served as the Department of Defense's manager for manned space flight support operations. This included command or operational control of all launch-area forces and recovery operations in support of Apollo missions and the launch of America's first orbiting space laboratory and its three-man crew.

In Craig Nelson's *The First Heroes*, Davey said this about his B-58 assignment: "I came home in 1955 and got orders up to Carswell AFB at Ft. Worth to run the B-58 Test Force, a four-engine delta-wing bomber. It was the first Mach-2 bomber, the first supersonic, and top secret; the plant where they built the aircraft was right across the runway. The aircraft was one big, huge fuel tank aerodynamically formed into a flying wing—sort of like a giant boomerang on wheels—and the atomic weapon was tucked inside that. It was my last flying assignment. That was a super job."

Jones attended the Command and General Staff School, Armed Forces Staff College, and the National War College. He retired from the air force in May 1973 as a major general. That same year, he accepted a civilian job with Southeast Banks and was chairman of the board of the Southeast Bank of Brevard when he again retired in 1982. In retirement, Gen. Jones was very active in community affairs. He participated in such groups as the chamber of commerce of South Brevard, Florida Institute of Technology, Florida Air Academy, United Way of Brevard County, American Cancer Society of Brevard, Holmes Regional Medical Center, and Brevard County Health Facility Authority

In July 1994, Gen. Jones moved to Texas and took up residence in Air Village II. In January 1999, he married Janna-Neen Cunningham—widow of long-time friend Gen. Joseph Cunningham. They split their living time between the Air Force Village in San Antonio and their home in Tucson, Arizona. Gen. Jones died of heart failure on November 25, 2008, at his home in Tucson. He was buried in Arlington National Cemetery along with his first wife, Anita.

RODNEY ROSS WILDER
Copilot

(There is some confusion over Wilder's correct name. Some books and Doolittle give it as Ross R. Wilder, while the War Department and others give it as Rodney Ross Wilder. The War Department version will be used here.)

Pre-Raid

"Hoss" Wilder was born January 10, 1917, at Taylor, Texas. He attended the University of Texas and Southwestern University, earning a BS in business administration. He entered military service in November 1940 as a flying cadet and graduated from flying training and was commissioned as a second lieutenant in May 1941. His first flying assignment was with the 95th Bomb Squadron, which was patrolling the West Coast for Japanese submarines. While flying as a copilot with "Brick" Holstrom, they located and sank a Japanese submarine at the mouth of the Columbia River.

Post-Raid

When Hoss bailed out of his B-25 in the rain and darkness, he landed safely on the side of a mountain in soft dirt. He spent the night on the mountain, warmed only by a pint of whiskey that he was able to stuff in his shirt as he bailed out. When daylight came, he heard a train and went down the mountain toward the sound. It was the village of Changsan, where Capt. David Jones had already arrived. They arranged for train transportation to Chuchow, where they joined up with other Raiders.

Following his escape from China, Hoss served as bombardment squadron commander in England, North Africa, Italy, and Corsica. He returned to the States in May 1944 and served as base commander in Texas and Oklahoma. He reverted to inactive reserve status in June 1947 and later became a regional director of the General Services Administration.

Wilder and his wife, Mildred, had two children—Susan and Morris. His highest rank held on active duty was colonel. He died of a heart attack at age forty-seven on June 6, 1964, and was buried at Taylor City Cemetery, Taylor, Texas.

EUGENE FRANCIS MCGURL
Navigator

Pre-Raid

Gene was born February 8, 1917, at Belmont, Massachusetts, into a staunch Catholic family that had eight children. Gene was an avid hockey player, good at math, congenial, and devoted to his family and country. He graduated from

Arlington High School, Arlington, Massachusetts, in 1934. He attended Northeastern University and then switched to MIT's School of Engineering for two years. He left MIT to join the army air corps in 1940, wanting to be a pilot. However, he washed out of pilot training, so he went into navigator training in Florida. After graduation and commissioning as a second lieutenant in December 1941, he was assigned to the 95th Bomb Squadron of the 17th Bombardment Group. When Pearl Harbor was bombed, Gene's unit moved to South Carolina, where he volunteered for Doolittle's secret mission. Gene was never married.

Post-Raid

Bad weather and low fuel caused Gene and his crew members to bail out near and southeast of Chuchow. During his escape through China, Gene and other Raiders spent some time hiding in a cave, waiting for airplane transportation. Sympathetic Chinese supplied them with paper and pencils, with which Gene wrote a diary of his recent experiences. He mailed this diary to his parents from Dinjan, India, and it has since been donated to a Doolittle museum in Texas. Lt. McGurl remained in the China-Burma-India theater after the Raid. He was killed in action on June 3, 1942, when his plane crashed into a mountain after bombing Lashio, Burma, en route to Kunming, China—only about six weeks after the Raid.

A memorial plaque for 1st Lt. McGurl was installed at Mt. Pleasant Cemetery, Arlington, Massachusetts, in July 1994. Another plaque honoring McGurl was installed on a bicycle path near the Grove St. Bridge in Arlington in May 1996.

DENVER VERNON TRUELOVE
Bombardier

Pre-Raid

Denver was born on April 10, 1919, at Clermont, Georgia. He graduated from Chattahoochee High School in Clermont then completed three years of college at what was then known as the Rabun Gap–Nacoochee Junior College. He studied vocational agriculture at the University of Georgia in Athens before he volunteered for the army air corps. He entered military service on May 13, 1940, at Atlanta, Georgia, and completed bombardier and navigator training in April 1941 and was commissioned a second lieutenant. His first assignment was as a B-25 bombardier with the 95th Bomb Squadron at Pendleton Field, Oregon, where he was selected for the Raid in February 1942.

Post-Raid

Denver bailed out over China with his crew members when their plane ran out of fuel. He reunited with all his crew members at Chunsien. After a few days, they all traveled by train and truck to Hengyang, then by C-47 to the safety of Chunking. After returning to the States, Truelove got a brief leave at his home in Lula, Georgia, and then was assigned to the North Africa campaign. He was killed in action at age twenty-three on April 5, 1943, while on a mission over Italy—about two years after the Raid. His flight was attacking an Axis shipping convoy in the Mediterranean Sea when his plane was hit by flak and crashed into the sea near Sicily; he died with the rank of captain. His remains were never found. Denver apparently had never been married. His only sister, Blanche Truelove Bowen, named her son after him.

JOSEPH WILLIAM MANSKE
Flight Engineer/Gunner

Pre-Raid

Joe was born on April 13, 1921, in Gowanda, New York—just southwest of Buffalo. He entered the army air corps in September 1939 at Chanute AFB, Illinois, and completed an aircraft mechanics course at Canute Field, Illinois. His first assignment was as a B-25 aircraft mechanic with the 95th Bomb Squadron at March Field, California, from July 1940 until he was selected for the Raid in February 1942.

The extra fuel tanks installed in the B-25s had improperly engineered seams, and the tanks leaked badly. On the way to the Japanese coast, Joe worried about the gas consumption. Like the other Raiders, he had been caught up in the excitement of the mission. C. V. Glines quotes Joe in *The Doolittle Raid* as later saying, "I gave little thought to just how dangerous a flight this would be. After we were into the flight for about thirty minutes we knew we wouldn't have enough gas to reach our destination. This was the first time that I fully realized what I'd gotten into. Being brought up in a good Christian home, I got down on my knees and prayed."

Post-Raid

Joe bailed out over China as his plane ran out of fuel, and he soon was returned to the States. He attended officer candidate school and was commissioned a second lieutenant in December 1942. He served in Africa and Italy as aircraft maintenance officer until 1945. He was released from active duty in April 1946 but was recalled to active duty with National Guard Affairs in March 1957. He had a combination of National Guard and air force assignments while serving at Brookley AFB, Alabama; Kelly AFB, Texas; White Plains, New York; and the Pentagon.

Joe's wife, Phyllis, was also born in Gowanda on March 19, 1922. They were married on October 20, 1945, and had two children: a daughter, Pamela (born in 1948), and a son, Mark (1951).

After serving thirty-two years in the military, Manske retired as a colonel in 1973. In his retirement, he became active full-time in the "Doolittle Tokyo Raiders Association," serving as president and CEO. He died at age seventy-six on April 4, 1998, and was buried at the Ft. Sam Houston National Cemetery, San Antonio, Texas.

Crew No. 6

Pilot.........................Lt. Dean E. Hallmark
Copilot.......................Lt. Robert J. Meder
Navigator.....................Lt. Chase J. Nielsen
Bombardier..................Sgt. William J. Dieter
Flight Engineer/Gunner..Sgt. Donald E. Fitzmaurice

DEAN EDWARD HALLMARK
Pilot

Pre-Raid

Dean was born on January 20, 1914, in Robert Lee, Texas. He graduated from Greenville High School, Greenville, Texas, and attended Paris Junior College in Texas and Polytechnic Institute in Alabama for two years. He played football while in college.

Dean entered the army in November 1940 at Houston. He graduated as pilot and was commissioned a second lieutenant from advanced flying school in Stockton, California, in July 1941. Dean joined the 95th Bomb Squadron at Pendleton, Oregon.

Lt. Hallmark was a husky man, 6 feet tall and 200 pounds, and was nicknamed "Jungle Jim." His Tokyo mission was to bomb steel mills in the northeastern section of Tokyo. Although they encountered heavy flak over Tokyo, they escaped the Raid without being hit. His plane was named *the "Green Hornet."*

Post-Raid

Dean flew on to the coast of China, where their fuel ran out. They decided to ditch in the ocean, and they had a fast and hard landing in the sea. The force of the crash landing ejected both Dean and his seat right through the windshield, leaving him badly cut, bruised, and barely able to walk. Dieter and Fitzmaurice were severely injured and drowned in the crash. Hallmark and the other two surviving crew members were initially helped by sympathetic Chinese, but one Chinese betrayed them to Japanese soldiers, so their attempted escape was short lived.

The Japanese took Hallmark and his two crew members and five other captured Raiders to Tokyo for torture and questioning. They were then taken back to China to the Kiangwan military prison, several miles outside Shanghai. After a mock trial, Hallmark, Farrow, and Spitzer were condemned to death. The men were allowed to write letters home to their families. Craig Nelson in *The First Heroes* quotes Dean's letter to his mother in Dallas: "I hardly know what to say. They have just told me that I am liable to execution. I can hardly believe it . . . I am a prisoner of war and I thought I would be taken care of until the end of the war . . . I did everything that the Japanese have asked me to do and tried to cooperate with them because I knew that my part in the war was over." The men were executed by firing squad at a cemetery near the prison on October 15, 1942. The bodies were cremated, and the ashes were placed in small boxes and put on an altar at the prison. Later, the boxes were removed and taken to the International Funeral Home in Shanghai, where they remained until the end of the war. They were later recovered and returned to the States for burial at Arlington National Cemetery, Virginia.

An interesting footnote occurred to Hallmark's story sixty years later. An army captain by the name of Adam Hallmark was watching the movie *Thirty Seconds over Tokyo* when he heard a reference in the movie to a "Hallmark." Having never known about Dean Hallmark, Adam Hallmark wondered if they might be related. A little genealogical detective work revealed that they were indeed distant cousins. Capt. Adam Hallmark—a squadron signal officer based at Ft. Hood, Texas—was touched and motivated by this discovery. He eagerly attended the next Raiders' reunion in 2006 and got to meet Chase Nielsen and other Raider survivors who knew his cousin. Adam is ensuring that his side of the family learns about Lt. Dean Hallmark and honors his memory.

ROBERT JOHN MEDER
Copilot

Pre-Raid
Robert was born on August 23, 1917, in Cleveland, Ohio. He graduated from Miami University of Ohio, where he was a member of Phi Kappa Tau fraternity and participated in track. He was in the aviation cadet flight school from 1940 to 1941 then was assigned to the 95th Bombardment Squadron of the 17th Bombardment Group in 1941. Robert then joined the secret Doolittle group in 1942.

Post-Raid
The Japanese captured Lt. Meder, along with the other two surviving members of his crew—Hallmark and Nielsen. He died of malnutrition and beriberi on December 11, 1943, while still in captivity. The Japanese cremated him, and his ashes were located after the war and returned home for burial in Arlington National Cemetery, Virginia, in 1949. The Arnold Air Society squadron at Miami University is named the Robert J. Meder Squadron in his memory.

Robert had written a letter to his family on the day of Pearl Harbor—to be opened in the event of his death (the letter is now posted on Todd Joyce's website, at www.doolittleraider.com). In one paragraph in the letter, Robert wrote: "The main purpose of this letter to you is to try at this very last minute to comfort you. During this time of strife for all, those of you that have had to sacrifice loved ones are the real heroes of any struggle. The word here is truly inadequate. Just remember that the soul of a person is greater than his own physical body; therefore, you have not lost me, my spirit shall ever be with you, watching, and aiding if possible from wherever the 'Great Beyond' may be. Be brave, not bitter, be determined, not overcome. That is the job for those of you that I love most dearly. Democracy shall continue. It is our sacrifice for that cause."

CHASE JAY NIELSEN
Navigator

Pre-Raid

Chase was born January 14, 1917, in Hyrum, Utah. He attended grade school and high school in Hyrum and graduated from South Cache High School in Hyrum in 1935. He then graduated from Utah State University with a BS in civil engineering in May 1939.

Chase entered the flying cadet program of the army air corps in August 1939 at Ft. Douglas in Salt Lake City, completing aerial navigation training, and was commissioned a navigator and second lieutenant in June 1941. He later earned ratings as senior aircraft observer and master navigator. In March 1942 he volunteered for the Doolittle mission.

Post-Raid

2nd Lt. Kelly Cahalan of the Ogden Air Logistics Complex described Chase's crash landing: "Nielsen and his crew ditched their bomber into the sea off the coast of China. He remembers his crew standing on top of the downed plane. Their life raft wouldn't inflate and they were unsuccessful in tying each other together before being swept away by the violent waves. 'The next thing I remember,' said Nielsen, 'I woke up on the coast thinking, 'What the heck am I doing here?'" The Japanese captured Nielsen and his two surviving crew members after their crash landing near the China coast. He experienced the same torture and interrogations as the other airmen, but he never broke. Chase described some of the tortures he endured in Craig Nelson's *The First Heroes*: "I was given what they call the water cure . . . I was put on my back on the floor with my arms and legs stretched out, one guard holding each limb. A towel was wrapped around my face and water was poured on. They poured water on this towel until I was almost unconscious from strangulation, then they would let up until I'd get my breath, then they'd start all over again. I felt more or less like I was drowning, just gasping between life and death. The guard then brought in a large bamboo pole about three inches in diameter. This was placed directly behind my knees. I was then made to squat on the floor in this position like a kneel. One guard had hold of each of my arms, one other guard then placed his foot on my thigh and would jump up and down causing severe pain to my knees. I felt that my joints were coming apart, but after about five minutes of that my knees were so numb I couldn't feel anything else."

He was kept prisoner for three and a half years and was sentenced to execution, but his sentence was later commuted to life imprisonment. Eventually, he was liberated by an OSS parachute rescue team a week after VJ day on the evening of August 20, 1945. He weighed only 103 pounds at the time. Of the eight Doolittle Raiders taken prisoner by the Japanese, three were executed, one died in captivity, and four (including Nielsen) were liberated at the end of the war. (Carroll V. Glines wrote a stirring book in 1981 about these four survivors, titled *Four Came Home*.) Just three months after his release, Nielsen returned to Shanghai, China, in January 1946 to testify and provide evidence at the international war crimes trials against his former captors. Nielsen was the only member of Crew No. 6 to survive the war.

Chase married Cleo McCrary of Portage, Utah, on July 17, 1946. They had two sons, Terry J. and Gregory B., and one daughter, Sherrie Lee. Cleo died February 5, 1995, from Alzheimer's disease. Chase married his second wife, Phyllis Henderson of Brigham City, Utah, on July 1, 1995. They enjoyed air shows, fishing, traveling, antique collecting, and gardening. Nielsen remained in the air force and rose through the ranks, helping to build up the Strategic Air Command. He became a member of SAC in March 1949 at Roswell AFB, New Mexico, where he was assigned to the 509th Bombardment Group—the first group to be organized, equipped, and trained for atomic warfare. During his decade with the major command, Col. Nielsen helped SAC develop key operational innovations, including radar navigation bombardment, air refueling employing the flying boom, and electronic countermeasures. He helped integrate "fail safe" and other emergency war order procedures into SAC's unique set of flight profiles. Col. Nielsen returned to the air while assigned to SAC and reached more than 10,000 flying hours, mostly in B-29s, B-50s, and B-52s. His longest flight lasted twenty-six hours nonstop without refueling from Okinawa, Japan, to Roswell, New Mexico, in a B-36. He retired in November 1961 as a lieutenant colonel and died on March 23, 2007, at his home in Brigham City, Utah, at the age of ninety. He was buried at the Hyrum City Cemetery, Hyrum, Utah.

WILLIAM JOHN DIETER
Bombardier

Pre-Raid

William was born October 5, 1912, at Vail, Iowa. He completed one year of high school then enlisted in the army on October 29, 1936, at Vancouver Barracks, Washington. He graduated from Coast Artillery Motor School, Ft. Lewis, Washington, in 1938. He reenlisted on December 12, 1940, with the 95th Bombardment Squadron, McChord Field, Washington. He transferred to Pendleton Field, Oregon, until his selection for the Raid in February 1942.

Post-Raid

Sgt. Dieter was killed during his crew's crash landing along the China coast. Evidently, he had been crushed upon impact when the brittle Plexiglas nose slammed into the water. His body was buried by the surviving crew members and some Chinese at Satow, China. After the war, Dieter's remains were recovered and reinterred at the Golden Gate National Cemetery in San Bruno, California, in 1949.

DONALD E. FITZMAURICE
Flight Engineer/Gunner

Pre-Raid
Donald was born March 13, 1919, in Lincoln, Nebraska. Not much is known about his life before entering the army. He struggled during the Depression with various odd jobs to make ends meet, and finally decided that the army air corps could provide a stable job environment. He enlisted in the army air corps in August 1940 and was trained as an aircraft mechanic at Chanute Field, Illinois, graduating in March 1941. His first assignment was to the 95th Bomb Squadron at McChord Field, Washington, where he served as a B-25 mechanic and flight engineer until he was selected for the Raid in February 1942.

Post-Raid
Donald died from his injuries during the crash landing on April 18, 1942, in the sea along the China coast, at the age of twenty-three. Both he and Dieter were severely injured in the crash and then were drowned in the heavy surf. Lt. Nielsen and the other two surviving crew members buried Fitzmaurice and Dieter on the beach. After the war, Lt. Nielsen was instrumental in recovering Fitzmaurice's remains, and they were reinterred in the Golden Gate National Cemetery in San Bruno, California.

About sixty years after the Raid, Kelly Estes—a sixteen- year-old grandniece to Fitzmaurice—created a touching oral history about her great uncle. She obtained a moving interview with Richard Fitzmaurice, Donald's brother. Richard was the last family member to see Donald alive, when Richard hitchhiked from his base in Greenville, Mississippi, to Eglin Field, Florida, to visit his brother shortly before the Raid. Shortly thereafter, Richard went on to fly as a navigator on B-17 bombing missions in Europe. He was shot down over Berlin on his thirteenth raid and was captured and imprisoned by the Germans for a year. Shortly after his capture, the Germans told him that his brother had been killed in China, but he refused to believe it at the time. Later, a new prisoner by the name of "Tokyo Jones" arrived at the prison and confirmed to Richard that his brother was indeed dead. This news was devastating to

Richard. It turns out that this "Tokyo Jones" was one of the Doolittle Raiders—Capt. David M. Jones. Jones had been shot down and captured over North Africa only three months after the Raid. It was an amazing coincidence that Jones ended up in the same German prison with Donald Fitzmaurice's brother. Kelly's story about her granduncle can be seen on the Stories of Service website at http://digiclub.org/sofs/. To find the story, click on "The Stories," then "All Stories," then do a "Basic Search" on "Donald Fitzmaurice."

Crew No. 7

```
Pilot..........................Lt. Ted W. Lawson
Copilot........................Lt. Dean Davenport
Navigator...................Lt. Charles L. McClure
Bombardier...................Lt. Robert S. Clever
Flight Engineer/Gunner......Cpl. David J. Thatcher
```

TED WILLIAM LAWSON
Pilot

Pre-Raid

Ted was born March 7, 1917, in Fresno, California. He attended schools in the Los Angeles area at Manual Arts High, Hollywood High, and Los Angeles City College. Ted met his future wife, Ellen Arlene Reynolds, while they both were students at Los Angeles City College. Ted majored in aeronautical engineering while working nights at Douglas Aircraft in the drafting department. He was very interested in aviation, so he jumped at the chance to join the flying cadets in 1940. Ted explains some of his thoughts in Craig Nelson's *The First Heroes*: "I was chucking a thirty-six-dollar-a-week job with a company that was beginning to get big war orders from abroad for a seventy-five-dollar-a-month job that might break my neck," Ted remembered. "But I wanted experience. I wanted to get my fingers into different kinds of planes and see how they worked. The army had those planes. The training period did something to me spiritually. It gave me my first real feeling of belonging to something; of being proud of being a part of a team. I knew that for me there would now be more than just taking something the army was offering. I'd want to be giving, too." He was sent off to Kelly and Randolph Fields in Texas for flight training. Upon completion of flight training and commissioning as a second lieutenant in November 1940, Ted was assigned to McChord Field in Washington. He spent much of his time ferrying planes from Douglas and North American to military air bases.

Ted and Ellen were married in Coeur d'Alene, Idaho, on September 5, 1941. After a three-month separation due to maneuvers in Mississippi, Ellen and Ted were enjoying a delayed honeymoon in Los Angeles when they heard the news on the radio about Pearl Harbor and the beginning of US involvement in World War II. Another separation followed and Ted was rushed back to Washington State to perform submarine patrol off the coast. Ted was soon reassigned to Columbia, South Carolina. He flew his B-25 to Columbia, while Ellen trailed behind in the family Buick. Before Ellen reached Columbia, she learned that Ted and some of his colleagues had been sent to Florida on a special mission. Ellen finally caught up with Ted again at Eglin Field in February, where he was already heavily involved in secret and urgent training. Ellen and Ted had only a month together in Eglin before it became time for the crews to fly to McClellan Field at Sacramento for final engine tuning before loading the planes onto the USS *Hornet* at Alameda Naval Base. The assumption was that the pilots would be gone for only about three months and would return to their new home base in Columbia, South Carolina. Ted flew his B-25—named the "*Ruptured Duck*"—to California, and Ellen decided to take up temporary residence in Myrtle Beach to await his return.

Post-Raid

Ted's plane ran out of fuel, and they decided to try to land on a Chinese beach. The plane flipped in a hard ocean landing. Ted suffered severe leg and facial injuries, resulting in a leg amputation in China and the loss of most of his front teeth. The shock of Ted's amputation and the severity of his other injuries caused him to remain in China longer than the other Raiders. He recuperated in a hospital in Linhai, while being tended by Dr. (Lt.) White. They got word from the Chinese underground that the Japanese were about to search their area, so they reluctantly made plans to move farther west. Ted was quoted in Craig Nelson's *The First Heroes*: "Before we left the grounds of the little hospital, the Chinese doctor came to my chair, smiling blandly. 'I want to show you something,' he said, and ordered my coolie to carry me around to the other side of the hospital. They set me down beside a coffin. It was a new one, made by the same Chinese carpenter who had made my crutches. It was to have been for me."

With the help of sympathetic Chinese, Lawson and his crew were able to successfully evade the Japanese search teams, and Ted was soon on his way back to the States by way of Cairo, Egypt. He and a few other Raiders were taken to Walter Reed Hospital in Washington, DC, to attend to their injuries. At the time, Ellen was temporarily in California, tending to Ted's mother, Mayne, who had experienced a stroke. Ted didn't want Ellen to see him in a damaged condition until he could be fitted with a prosthesis and could walk again. However, Gen. Doolittle played Cupid and arranged for a surprise reunion for Ted and Ellen at Walter Reed.

While Ted was confined to the hospital, he occupied himself with documenting his firsthand experience and knowledge of the formerly secret Tokyo Raid. He decided to write a book since he felt so strongly about wanting the world to know the terrible sacrifices many Chinese made in helping the American flyers evade capture by the humiliated Japanese. Ted obtained the services of well-known newspaper columnist Bob Considine (1906–75) to help him write the book *Thirty Seconds over Tokyo*. The book was published in 1943 on the first anniversary of the Tokyo Raid. Hollywood studios competed over the rights to make the movie version. Roughly half the book is about the Raid, and the other half is about the wartime love story of Ted and Ellen. The book and the movie derivative quickly became highly acclaimed accounts of the historic Doolittle Raid.

While in Walter Reed Hospital, Ted got to meet President Franklin D. Roosevelt and Mrs. Roosevelt. The president's wife, Eleanor, took a strong liking to Ted and Ellen—a friendship that lasted over many years after the war. By the time Ted got out of the hospital, he was tired of the publicity about the Raid and the book and the movie, so he asked for an overseas assignment.

While still in the army, he got a job in one of President Roosevelt's favorite projects—the Lend Lease program—and was assigned to Santiago, Chile, as liaison officer with the US Air Mission. He finally got out of the army air corps in February 1945, and his and Ellen's life started to return to civilian normalcy. They had two daughters and one son. Their first daughter, Arlene Ann, was born in 1942, while Ted was recuperating at Walter Reed. The second daughter, Kathryn Jo, came in 1944, and their son, Robert William, was born in 1948. Ted worked for several corporations, including a twelve-year stint with Reynolds Metals, finally retiring to Chico, California, around 1965. Ted continued to fly, but in small civilian aircraft. He used his cane to help control the rudder pedals in place of his missing leg. Ted died January 19, 1992, just a few months after their fiftieth wedding anniversary, and he is buried in the Chico Cemetery.

Ellen continued to live in their family home in a peaceful walnut orchard on the outskirts of Chico until she died on February 5, 2009. She had been an inveterate collector of Doolittle Raid memorabilia, and she was very active in keeping up correspondence with the surviving Raiders, their families, and military historians. Her over sixty-year collection of Raider biographies, obituaries, newspaper clippings, and correspondence has formed the basis of this book.

DEAN DAVENPORT
Copilot

Pre-Raid
Dean was born June 29, 1918, in Spokane, Washington. He grew up in the Portland area and graduated from Portland High School. He attended Albany College (now Lewis and Clark College) and Northwestern School of Law in Portland before enlisting as a flying cadet in February 1941. Dean graduated from advanced flying school and was commissioned a second lieutenant in September 1941. His first assignment was as a B-25 pilot with the 95th Bomb Squadron at Pendleton Field, Oregon, where he remained until he was selected for the Raid in February 1942.

Post-Raid
Along with Lt. Lawson, Lt. Davenport was ejected through the windshield when their B-25 crash-landed in the ocean. Dean also suffered a severe leg injury in the crash. After escaping through China, Davenport returned to the States for his recovery. He served as technical advisor for the movie *Thirty Seconds over Tokyo*, and he elected to stay in the army air corps. Craig Nelson

reports in *The First Heroes* that when MGM approached the War Department for a stunt pilot on the picture *A Guy Named Joe*, the army recommended Davenport. He returned to combat in the Korean War, flying eighty-six missions as a fighter pilot. At one time, he was wing commander of the 4756th Air Defense Wing, Tyndall AFB, Florida. Dean was a graduate of the Air Command and Staff College, Maxwell AFB, Alabama. Dean had many operational and command assignments in such locations as Ft. Slocum, New York; Shaw AFB, South Carolina; South Korea; Moody AFB, Georgia; Randolph AFB, Texas; Tyndall AFB, Florida; Japan; and McChord AFB, Washington. His last assignment was as commander of the Boston Air Defense Sector at Hancock Field in New York from 1965 until his retirement as a colonel in September 1967.

Dean met his wife, Mary Lowry, when she was the executive secretary to the chief executive officer in the Office of Price Administration. Mary attended the University of South Carolina and was descended from a pre–Revolutionary War family. They had four children: Dean Jr. (born in 1944), Mary Lee (Mimi) (1948), Julia Lowry (1949), and Stephen Hugh (1955.)

Dean retired as a colonel in 1967. He died February 14, 2000, in Panama City, Florida, at age eighty-one. His wife, Mary, died January 11, 2003. He was buried at the Barrancas National Cemetery in Pensacola, Florida.

CHARLES LEE MCCLURE
Navigator

Pre-Raid
"Mac" McClure was born October 4, 1916, in St. Louis, Missouri. He graduated from University High School, University City, Ohio, and attended the University of Missouri. He enlisted as a flying cadet on October 12, 1940, at Jefferson Barracks, Missouri, and graduated from navigator training and was commissioned as a second lieutenant on December 5, 1941—two days before the Japanese bombed Pearl Harbor.

Post-Raid
Mac's shoulders were severely injured in the crash landing of his plane. Upon his return to the States, he spent nine months undergoing repair and treatment at Walter Reed Hospital for his fractured shoulders. His weight had dropped from 205 down to 139. He met and married his occupational therapist—Betty Jean Buchanan. Upon his release from Walter Reed in June 1943, Mac was assigned duties as a navigator instructor. However, complications from his crash injuries again hospitalized him from February until June 1945, when he

was retired on a physical disability. Mac then began a civilian career as a service representative with Appleton Wire Works in Appleton, Wisconsin.

Charles and Betty had five children: Wendy, Charles Lee Jr., Margaret, and Cory. Betty died in 1981, and later that same year, Mac married his second wife, Edith Goodell Sairs. Edith had two children from her prior marriage: George T. Sairs Jr. and Sandra Sairs McDonald.

Mac and Edith moved to Tucson, Arizona, where Mac died at age eighty-two on January 19, 1999. He was cremated and his ashes were scattered over military grounds.

ROBERT STEVENSON CLEVER
Bombardier

Pre-Raid
Robert was born May 22, 1914, in Portland, Oregon. He enlisted as an aviation cadet at Vancouver Barracks, Washington, on March 15, 1941. He was commissioned a second lieutenant with rating as bombardier on December 16, 1941, at Pendleton Field, Oregon. His first assignment was as a B-25 bombardier with the 95th Bomb Squadron at McChord Field, Washington, from December 1941 until he was selected for the Raid in February 1942.

Post-Raid
Clever was thrown through the Plexiglas nose of the B-25 upon impact and severely injured. After escaping through China, he was sent back to the States and was stationed at Ft. Wayne, Indiana. After recovering from his injuries, he served as a B-26 navigator with the 432nd Bomb Squadron at Barksdale Field, Louisiana. Just six months after the Raid, he was killed on November 20, 1942, when his B-26 crashed near Versailles, Ohio, due to engine failure. Robert was buried at the Lincoln Memorial Park Cemetery in Portland, Oregon.

DAVID JONATHAN THATCHER
Flight Engineer/Gunner

Pre-Raid
David was born July 31, 1921, in Bridger, Montana, and graduated from Absarokee High School in 1939. He enlisted in the army at Billings, Montana, and was sworn into the army air corps at Ft. Missoula, Montana, on December 3, 1940. He first went to McChord Field in Tacoma for basic training then was assigned to the 95th Bomb Squadron, 17th Group. In the spring of 1941, the

17th Group went to Pendleton, Oregon, then on maneuvers to Felts Field at Spokane. His next assignment was to airplane mechanics school at Lincoln, Nebraska. After completion of school, the 17th Group was moved to Columbia, South Carolina, where David volunteered for the Doolittle mission. It was then on to Eglin Field in Florida for quick mission training.

Post-Raid

The crash landing in the sea knocked Thatcher unconscious, but he quickly recovered and found himself uninjured. He was able to wade ashore and was instrumental in giving life-saving first aid to his injured crew members. He played a key role in helping his colleagues escape the Japanese pursuers. Gen. Doolittle made sure that Thatcher received a Silver Star for his gallantry and dedication to the safety of his crew members at great risk to himself.

After returning to the States, Thatcher was assigned to MacDill AFB at Tampa, Florida, for training on Martin B-26s in the 320th Group. In early October 1942, he boarded the converted *Queen Mary* troop ship in New York for an Atlantic crossing to Glasgow, Scotland. He was sent to Oran, Algeria, where he flew twenty-six missions against the Germans in a B-26, including the first raid on Rome. David returned to the States in January 1944 and was stationed at March Field and Victorville, California, flying B-24s. He was discharged in July 1945 and returned to his home in Montana. David married Dawn Goddard on December 22, 1945, in Billings, and they had five children during their seventy-year marriage: Sandra Jean, born in 1947; Gary, in 1949 (killed in Vietnam in 1970); Becky, in 1952; Jeff, in 1955; and Debra Dawn, in 1962, who passed away in June 2009 from complications due to brain cancer.

David attended the University of Montana for three years and had a career with the US Postal Service until he retired in 1980. David died of a stroke at age ninety-four on June 22, 2016, in Missoula, Montana. He was buried with full military honors at the Sunset Memorial Gardens in Missoula. He was the next-to-last surviving Raider.

Crew No. 8

Pilot........................Capt. Edward J. York
Copilot......................Lt. Robert G. Emmens
Navigator/Bombardier ....Lt. Nolan A. Herndon
Flight Engineer..........S.Sgt. Theodore H. Laban
Gunner.......................Sgt. David W. Pohl

EDWARD JOSEPH YORK
Pilot

Pre-Raid

Edward was born August 16, 1912, in Batavia, New York, with the surname of Cichowski. He changed his name to York while he was in flight school because so many people had trouble pronouncing or spelling it. His nickname was "Eddy" during childhood but became "Ski" to his military friends. His father was a Polish immigrant who came to America in 1905. Eddy graduated from Batavia High School in June 1928 at the age of fifteen and was remembered as an excellent student and especially gifted in mathematics. He had a long-standing desire to go to West Point, so he enlisted in the army infantry in July 1930 as his best avenue to win an appointment to the academy. He served in several posts, including Chilkoot Barracks, Alaska, before being selected for an academy preparation school in San Francisco. After three years as an enlisted man, Ski won his academy admission via a congressional appointment by Sen. Hiram Johnson in California.

During his West Point career, Ski planned to enter the cavalry. However, he changed his mind upon graduation when he learned that cavalry officers were required to buy about $2,000 of special uniforms while pilots had to buy only one shirt and one pair of pants. He quickly changed his field to aviation, and he was sent off to flying school at San Antonio, Texas. He initially entered fighter training, but he was diverted into bomber training because of a new height restriction for fighter pilots of 5 feet 10 inches. He met his future wife, Mary Elizabeth Harper, while in San Antonio, and they were married on August 28, 1939. Ski's first assignment after flight school was to March Field, California, in the 17th Attack Group, which later became the 17th Bombardment Group. The 17th was moved to McChord Field, Tacoma, Washington, and they were equipped with B-25s at the time Pearl Harbor came along. The 17th was then transferred to Columbia, South Carolina, with the rumor that they would prepare for assignment to England to help fight the Germans. By this time, Ski was a captain and a squadron commander. One afternoon in Columbia, Lt. Col. Doolittle arrived on the base and told the group commander that he wanted to meet the four squadron commanders. When he got everybody behind closed doors, he announced that he was going to bomb Tokyo, and he wanted the squadron commanders to ask for volunteers for a dangerous, top-secret assignment. The 17th Bombardment Group was targeted for volunteers because they had the most experience with B-25s, which was selected as the most feasible medium-range bomber to use for the mission. Although the squadron commanders could not divulge the target, they had no problem getting more than enough volunteers. They all were soon on their way to Eglin Field for short-takeoff training.

When the planes and crews got to McClelland Field in California for final engine checks and were ready to go to Alameda for loading on the USS *Hornet*, York's plane was experiencing severe backfiring because the maintenance crews had incorrectly replaced the specially modified carburetors—not knowing of the secret mission and the need for extreme fuel efficiency. York and Doolittle decided to proceed with the plane, even though it was not expected to get optimum fuel efficiency.

Initially, York was not intended to be a pilot on the mission. Theoretically, Doolittle had just "borrowed" him to be a temporary operations officer while the group was training at Eglin. However, York desperately wanted to go on the mission, and at the last minute he somehow wheedled his way into commanding one of the B-25s. York asked Lt. Bob Emmens to be his copilot, and they quickly assembled a crew for their plane.

Post-Raid

The flight from the carrier to Japan had taken about five hours. By the time York's plane got to Japan, he and his crew realized that their fuel-guzzling aircraft wasn't going to have enough range left to reach China. As an alternative, they decided to head for Russia, which was closer and was a neutral country. They continued to fly toward Russia until they had just about thirty or forty minutes of fuel left, then they started looking for a place to land. York knew the Russians were anti-Japanese, and he thought it would be a safe refuge even though the crews had been warned not to land in Russia, since Russia didn't want to alienate the Japanese while they were busy fighting the Germans.

York and his crew landed about 40 miles north of Vladivostok and were interned in Russia for thirteen months. York and his crew got bored doing nothing while under house arrest, so on a lark, he mailed a letter to Joseph Stalin asking if he and his crew could be put to some useful purpose, such as fighting with the Russians, or being put in a training role, or, at a minimum, being moved to a warmer climate and be allowed to work. Much to York's surprise, a couple of Russian officers showed up a few weeks later to tell him that Stalin had granted his request to be moved to a warmer climate. On the train to the new location at Ashkahabad on the Soviet-Iranian border, York met a guy on the train who offered to put him in touch with some smugglers who could help them escape from Russian captivity. York and his crew took advantage of this offer and soon found themselves across the border into Persia (Iran), and then back to freedom in the States via India. York always thought that the Russians purposely let them escape, but Emmens always disagreed, insisting that their escape was due only to their good fortune and careful planning. York and his crew had received high priority for their transportation back to the States, but it still took a tiring seven-day journey via Yeman, India,

Iran, Oman, Ethiopia, Nigeria, Sudan, Lagos, Ascension Island, Brazil, and several other refueling stops in South America.

Over the years, a mystery theory has developed about York's plane going to Russia. Some people have believed that York and his copilot Emmens had secret orders to land in Russia after the Raid on Tokyo. No evidence has ever been found to confirm this theory (more on this mystery follows in Emmens's biography below).

After R & R in the States, York was sent to Ft. Worth, Texas, to transition into B-24s. However, he was shortly recruited by an old friend to become his deputy in a new B-17 group being formed to go to Europe. After about three months' training at MacDill Field in Florida, they moved to Italy in February 1944 to join the 15th Air Force. Over the next six months, York had sixteen official missions before he got grounded because of a new policy that all Doolittle Raider veterans, ex-internees, and ex-escapees could no longer fly combat missions. York was sent back to Randolph Field in Texas in a training capacity. However, six months later he got a chance to go to Poland to work in the US embassy. In 1947, York left Poland and returned to the States as commandant of the Officer Candidate School at Lackland AFB, Texas. After that, a tour followed in Copenhagen as air attaché at the American Embassy for three years. Next, he was assigned to the Air War College at Maxwell AFB in 1951. Following the War College, he became head of the attaché branch for three years, picking the air attachés for fifty-three stations around the world. Then he became deputy chief of staff for plans at the Military Air Transport Service (MATS). His final two assignments were with Titan missiles and then the Security Service. He retired as a colonel in 1968 with over thirty years of service.

Ski and wife, Mary, had two children: Tekla Ann (Tina), born in 1942, and Edward Joseph (Joe), born in 1947. Tina married William Daniel—a doctor—and she worked in the medical field. Joe graduated from the Air Force Academy in 1970 and was a navigator for a while, then he became a lawyer, but he died of cancer in 1996. Joe was married to Joanne Fyda.

In July 1984, the air force conducted an oral-history interview with York, resulting in a seventy-seven-page report published by the US Air Force Historical Research Center (K239.0512.1592). York died of a heart attack at his home in San Antonio on August 31, 1984, at age seventy-two. He was buried at Ft. Sam Houston National Cemetery in San Antonio.

ROBERT GABEL EMMENS
Copilot

Pre-Raid

Bob was born July 22, 1914, in Medford, Oregon. Bob's father was a physician, and Bob initially planned a medical career, but he changed his mind and entered the army in 1937 at Vancouver Barracks, Washington, following the death of his father. He became a flying cadet at Randolph Field, Texas. On December 7, 1941, he was flying over the Grand Canyon when he heard a radio commentator report the bombing of Pearl Harbor. "At first, the crew thought it was a fake," he recalled. "Another Orson Welles broadcast." His unit was first assigned to submarine patrol duty on Puget Sound, and his squadron was credited with sinking one of the first Japanese subs in that area. Shortly after Emmen's unit was transferred to Columbia, South Carolina, he and others volunteered for Doolittle's secret mission. However, Bob never got sent to Eglin, so he missed the secret training. He was left behind in Columbia to command the men not selected to go to Eglin for the training. Capt. York was operations officer at Eglin, and he likewise didn't go through the Raid training. Emmens's son Michael later heard the story that York called Emmens in Columbia and told him to bring another B-25 down to Eglin to pick up York, and they flew west as a replacement plane. However, York and Emmens and their B-25 got loaded onto the USS *Hornet*, and they became crew no. 8 in the Raid. The beginning of a mystery!

Nolan Herndon promoted the theory that York and Emmens had been given secret orders to go on the Raid and to land in Russia—a partial explanation for why they didn't get the short-field training in Eglin. Emmens's son Michael recently said that he asked his Dad several times why he didn't go through the training, and his answer was always "Just lucky, I guess." Michael had a couple of other interesting points to mention regarding Herndon's secret-orders theory:

1. About March 15—just a month before the Raid—the highest-ranking navigator—Tom Griffin—and Pilot Davy Jones were sent from Eglin to the War Department in Washington to obtain navigation and targeting information for the Raid. While there, they ran into York and Emmens in the cafeteria. When asked what they were doing there, York and Emmens refused to say.
2. After bombing their targets and discovering their high fuel burn rate, the decision was made to head for Russia. York then gave Herndon a map of Russia. Herndon stated later that he discovered in talking to other crews that no other crew had been issued a map of Russia.

Michael knows several people who have tried to research Herndon's theory, including searching Gen. Hap Arnold's files at the Library of Congress, and they couldn't find anything concrete. On several occasions, Michael talked to C. V. Glines, an honorary Raider and their official historian, and asked him about the theory. Glines stated that he asked Doolittle if crew no. 8 had orders to go to Russia, and Doolittle's response was "Well, if they did, I didn't give them." But he never outright confirmed or denied the rumor. Michael has come to believe Herndon's theory as the only plausible explanation for these intriguing facts.

Bob married his wife, Justine, on October 14, 1939, in Medford, and they had three children: Thomas in 1942, Robin in 1945, and Michael in 1947. Thomas pursued an advanced degree in political science, and Michael first had a career in business management then pursued a second career in his first love of medicine. He became a critical-care nurse, working as a flight nurse on an air ambulance, both helicopters and fixed wing.

Craig Nelson points out in his book *The First Heroes* that the crew of plane 8 had the most reason to be nervous about the takeoff from the *Hornet*. Their pilot, Ski York, had been so overwhelmed by his officer's duties in helping Doolittle with the mission's behind-the-scenes prep work that he had missed out on the Eglin training, as had his copilot, Bob Emmens. "The ship shuddered under the strain of both throttles thrown wide open; flaps were down; controls all the way back in our laps," Emmens remembered. "York released his brakes and we began to roll, left wheel on the white line, down the deck of the carrier, slowly at first—my God, how slowly! Then faster, faster—the island of the carrier was lost from sight as it passed a bare eight feet away from our right wingtip; and then, like a big living thing, our plane seemed to leap into the air just as the deck of the ship disappeared under us and was replaced by the frothing sea."

Post-Raid

Emmens's plane was the only plane in the Raid that landed safely. They landed in Russia, since they didn't have enough fuel to reach China. He and his crew were interned for about thirteen months. After escaping from Russia via Iran, Emmens decided to stay with the military for a career, and he spent most of his years in intelligence.

Bob's assignments carried him to Bucharest, Romania (1944), the Pentagon (1948), air force intelligence in Salisbury, Austria (1951), Langley Field, Virginia (1957), air attaché in Tokyo, Japan (1958), and OSI at McChord AFB (1963). Bob's son Michael told the author: "When Dad received his orders for his assignment as air attaché to Japan, he was filled with trepidation that his being a Doolittle Raider would be held against him and our family. I was warned to keep that knowledge close to the vest. There were times when we were accosted by individuals that were angry at us because of World War II, but those incidents were rare. More serious was the rise of the *Zengakuren*, a student pro-communist, anti-American group. In the early 1960s, Francis Gary Powers was shot down in his U-2 spy plane over Russia. A forged letter bearing Dad's signature appeared, presumably giving permission for the plane to take off from Japan. It didn't. It took off from Turkey. But before the letter was proved a forgery, it caused massive anti-American demonstrations in Japan. This caused Eisenhower to cancel a planned visit to Japan. But since his advance team and equipment were already in the country, we got to go for a ride in the Marine 1 helicopter. Despite any incidents, Dad and I came to realize the Japanese people were extremely humble, polite, gracious, friendly, and nothing like the image of the people once portrayed as an enemy. Dad came to realize the enemy in World War II was not the people of Japan, but the government. This sentiment pervaded his thinking for the rest of his life."

While serving in Romania, he gave flying lessons to the nineteen-year-old king of Romania—King Michael I, after whom son Michael was named. Bob was a graduate of the command and staff school, Ft. Leavenworth, Kansas. He spent 1962 with tuberculosis at Fitzsimmons Hospital in Denver. Bob retired from the air force as a colonel in 1964 and settled back in Medford. Col. Emmens wrote an interesting book about his experience as a captive in Russia, titled *Guests of the Kremlin*—first published in 1949. In addition, he left an unpublished manuscript titled *Romania: Rape of a Nation*. After the military, Emmens worked in Medford as a stockbroker and in real estate. He also taught courses in conversational Japanese at Southern Oregon University and pursued his lifelong love for playing the piano every chance he could. He died of cancer on April 2, 1992, at age of seventy-seven. Justine died in January 2006. Bob, Justine, and their oldest son, Thomas, all are buried in the IOOF Eastwood Cemetery in Medford, Oregon.

NOLAN ANDERSON HERNDON
Navigator/Bombardier

Pre-Raid
Nolan was born December 12, 1918, in Greenville, Texas. He attended two years of college at Texas A&M University then enlisted in the army in Dallas on July 27, 1940. He was commissioned as a second lieutenant on June 24, 1941, and received both bombardier and navigator training.

Post-Raid

Herndon returned to the States in May 1943, where he held several assignments until the end of World War II. He retired from active duty on November 4, 1945. He married Julia Crouch—a relative of another Raider—Lt. Horace Crouch. They had two children, Nolan A. Jr. and James M. In civilian life, Herndon raised cattle and went into the wholesale grocery business in Edgefield, South Carolina.

Late in life, Herndon—by then the sole survivor of his plane's crew—began sharing his theory that his plane had been on a secret mission to purposely land in Russia after the Raid in order to test Russia's willingness to help the Americans in their war against Japan. At the time, Russia was holding on to neutrality with Japan, since they were heavily involved with war with Germany and they couldn't handle two major conflicts at the same time. To bolster this theory, Herndon mentioned several suspicious facts:

1. His plane had been selected to go on the Raid at the last minute, and York and Emmens were very late additions to the team and did not have the same training as the other crew members.
2. He claimed that both York and Emmens were fluent in Russian, and that later they both held high positions in military intelligence.
3. The specially modified carburetors that had been installed in Eglin were replaced by maintenance crews at McClellan with standard, less efficient models, but no record had been made of the substitution. According to Herndon's presumption, the higher fuel consumption would give a plausible excuse for having to divert to Russia rather than heading for China.

No other military person has ever confirmed Herndon's theory about the Russian "secret mission." The pilot—Edward York—was a very close friend with Ted Lawson, and he told Lawson many years ago that there was absolutely no truth to the story. In his book *Guests of the Kremlin*, Emmens made it clear that they didn't start learning Russian until they were interned in Russia.

Maj. Herndon died of pneumonia at age eighty-eight at the William Jennings Bryan Dorn VA Medical Center in Columbia, South Carolina, on October 7, 2007. He was buried in the Travis Park Cemetery in Saluda, South Carolina.

THEODORE H. LABAN
Flight Engineer

Pre-Raid

Ted was born July 13, 1914, in Kenosha, Wisconsin. He graduated from Kenosha High School and entered the army on October 12, 1935, at Vancouver Barracks, Washington. He first trained as an aircraft gunner and joined the army air corps in October 1938, completing maintenance courses on B-25, B-26, and B-29 aircraft. He became a flight engineer in 1940, serving with the 95th Bomb Squadron in California, Washington, and Oregon before being selected for the Raid in early 1942.

Post-Raid

After the thirteen-month internment in Russia, Ted returned to the States and joined the 496th Bomb Squadron at Hunter Field, Florida, and went with the squadron to England in January 1944, where he served as a flight engineer on B-26 Marauders. After the war, Ted served as flight engineer on B-29 and B-36 bombers, serving at bases in the Philippines, Guam, California, Maine, and Texas. He married Mary Elizabeth (surname unknown). His final assignment was with the 3513th Combat Crew Training Squadron at Randolph AFB, Texas, where he retired as a master sergeant on November 30, 1956. After military retirement, he earned his BS in electrical engineering and worked as a research engineer. Ted died on September 16, 1998, in Hot Springs, Arkansas, and was buried at Highland Cemetery, Ozark, Arkansas.

DAVID WILLIAM POHL
Gunner

Pre-Raid

Dave was born December 31, 1921, in Boston, Massachusetts. He grew up in Wellesley, Massachusetts, and graduated from Wellesley High School in 1939. He entered the army air corps in January 1940 at Boston. He was believed to be the youngest crew member (age twenty) of the eighty who took part in the Raid.

Post-Raid

After escaping from Russia after thirteen months of internment, Pohl attended pilot training in August 1945. He served in the Training Command and

Caribbean Defense Command in Panama, Canal Zone. He was a copilot on a B-17 and later graduated to the left (pilot) seat, and in time to aircraft commander. He left the military in 1947 after eight years of service.

After the military, Pohl earned his BS degree in business administration from Babson Institute in Boston in 1951, then he worked as a marketing analyst specializing in industrial products. He later worked for an aircraft company but was working for Shell Oil Company when he retired in San Diego. Dave apparently never married. In his retirement years, he enjoyed taking train vacations and ocean cruises. Pohl died on February 18, 1999. He was cremated, with his ashes scattered in the Pacific Ocean.

Crew No. 9

Pilot.........................Lt. Harold F. Watson
Copilot...................Lt. James M. Parker Jr.
Navigator...................Lt. Thomas C. Griffin
Bombardier..................Sgt. Wayne M. Bissell
Flight Engineer/Gunner......T.Sgt. Eldred V. Scott

HAROLD FRANCIS WATSON
Pilot

Pre-Raid

"Doc" Watson was born in Buffalo, New York, on April 3, 1916, but he spent his youth in Hartford, Connecticut, attending William H. Hall High School in West Hartford. While there, he was a member of the football team, track team, rifle team, glee club, band, and orchestra. He attended Virginia Military Institute for a year and then transferred to Norwich University at Northfield, Vermont, where he completed most of his senior year before leaving school to enlist as a flying cadet. He completed flight training and was commissioned a second lieutenant in September 1940. At VMI, he played football and was a member of the freshman boxing and track teams. At Norwich, he was a member of the school's excellent horse polo team, as well as a member of Theta Chi fraternity, the drill team, and the interfraternity track team. He was class president and president of the Maroon Key. He majored in science and literature and was in the 1940 yearbook. (Norwich was the first private military college in the country, established in 1819, and the birthplace of ROTC.)

Doc's plane—named the "*Whirling Dervish*"—almost missed the takeoff from the *Hornet*. Watson had authorized Sgt. Scott to replace the spark plugs in the left engine because they were fouled. They were not scheduled to take off until later, so he felt he had plenty of time to do the maintenance. However, the unexpected early launch caught them off guard, and when the departure alarm sounded, Watson found the cowling off the left engine and all the plugs removed. Fortunately, since Watson's plane didn't have to take off until about thirty minutes after Doolittle's first departure, they had time to scramble and get everything back together just in time for their takeoff. Watson's plane hit Tokyo with three demolition bombs and one incendiary cluster.

Post-Raid

The crew noticed they had a fuel leak in the bottom tank where the lower turret had been removed, so Watson knew they wouldn't have enough range to reach their safe-destination base in China. He let the crew help decide their emergency backup plan. If they ran out of fuel over water, they planned to fly as long as possible, then find and strafe a small boat, ditch beside it, take it over, and try to make their way on to a safe port. However, Watson's careful conservation of fuel allowed them to reach mainland China before their fuel ran out. It was too dark and rainy to allow for a landing, so they were forced to bail out about 100 miles south of Poyang Lake. All crew members except Watson reached the ground without injury; he had selected a parachute too small for him. When it opened, it broke his arm and almost pulled it out of the socket.

Watson and his crew stayed with sympathetic Chinese in a mountain village then started a trek out of the area. Watson had to be carried by Chinese porters until they reached Hengyang, where they got transportation to Chunking. Watson was quickly evacuated to the States and spent considerable time recuperating at Walter Reed Hospital along with Ted Lawson. After the Raid, Watson was promoted to captain. His home was in West Hartford, Connecticut. By that time, he had been married two years, but little was recorded about his wife, Gene, or family. Doc served at many bases from 1943 to 1961, including Gowan Field, Idaho; Atlantic City, New Jersey; Peterson Field, Colorado; Spokane Field, Washington; Bolling AFB, Washington, DC; Hunter AFB, Georgia; Japan; Barksdale AFB, Louisiana; Turner AFB, Georgia; and Tinker AFB, Oklahoma. He attended the Air Command and Staff College in 1952 at Maxwell AFB, Alabama. His last assignment was at George AFB, California, where he retired as a lieutenant colonel in 1961. No information on his later career has been found. He died at age seventy-five on September 14, 1991, in Inglewood, California, where he was cremated.

JAMES MONROE PARKER JR.
Copilot

Pre-Raid

Jim was born February 4, 1920, in Houston, Texas. His family moved to Livingston, Texas, in 1931. He graduated from Livingston High School in 1938, where he was an athlete who excelled in football and baseball. He attended Lon Morris Junior College and Texas A&M. Jim enlisted in the army air corps in Houston in November 1940. He was sent to Stockton, California, and graduated from advanced flying school, class 41-E, as a pilot in July 1941. He was assigned to the 17th Bombardment Group in Pendleton, Oregon, where he volunteered for the Doolittle Raid—not knowing what the target was. He was transferred to South Carolina, where he received special training.

Post-Raid

Jim said that the only injury he received during the war was when he bailed out over China after bombing Tokyo. He pulled the ripcord too hard and knocked himself out. He landed in a tree after bailing out when the plane's fuel ran out over China. He stayed the night in the tree and climbed down in the morning. During his walk, he came across Tom Griffin and Eldred Scott—they traveled together and were commandeered by some provincial Chinese soldiers. Later, Harold Watson and Eric Bissell joined the group. The Chinese aided their escape from the Japanese into free China. Jim, along with his crew, was transferred out of China on May 14, 1942. During his time in China, Jim contracted malaria and was transferred to Walter Reed Hospital in Washington, DC, upon his return to the States. He, along with Harold Watson, Charles McClure, Ted Lawson, and Howard Sessler, all received treatment at Walter Reed at the same time.

After recovering at Walter Reed, Jim served in North Africa as a pilot of B-26 light bombardment aircraft. He was assigned to the 432nd Bomber Squadron, 17th Bomb Group, in North Africa from December 1942 until November 1943. During this time, he piloted twenty-six sorties. He returned to the States and was stationed at Battle Creek, Michigan, where he met Vonda Louden, whom he married in June 1944. After World War II, he served in Europe in the Army of Occupation from 1946 to 1947, along with his wife, Vonda, and new son, Jimbo. Jim returned to the States and was assigned to Oklahoma City for training. He separated from the service in June 1947, but he remained in the Air Force Reserves and attained the rank of lieutenant colonel. After leaving the service, Jim worked in the auto parts business in various cities around Texas: Livingston, Alpine, Monahans, New Braunfels, San Angelo, and Houston, until his retirement in 1987. He and Vonda had two children: Robert John and James Monroe IV (Jimbo). Jimbo was injured in a football accident in 1961, causing him to become a paraplegic, which was devastating to Jim and Vonda. Jim was proud to be a part of the Doolittle Raid and considered all the Raiders and their families part of his family. Jim and Vonda attended most of the Doolittle reunions until Jim's death from renal failure on June 19, 1991. He was buried at Restland Memorial Park, Livingston, Texas. After Jim's death, Vonda continued to attend the reunions until her death in February 2006. She is buried alongside Jim at Restland Memorial Park.

THOMAS CARSON GRIFFIN
Navigator

Pre-Raid

Tom was born July 10, 1916, in Green Bay, Wisconsin. He graduated from the University of Alabama with a BA in political science in 1939. He entered the military upon graduation from ROTC in July 1939 as a second lieutenant in the coast artillery, but he requested relief from active duty in 1940 to enlist as a flying cadet. He was rated as a navigator and recommissioned July 1, 1940. He was assigned to the 17th Bombardment Group in Pendleton, Oregon. Immediately after Pearl Harbor, his group began submarine patrols off the Oregon and Washington coasts. In February 1942, he volunteered for the classified Doolittle mission and was transferred to Columbia, South Carolina, and then on to Eglin Field. Griffin was one of the few crew members who knew the true destination of the Raid before they left Eglin. Both he and Lt. David Jones had been sent to Washington, DC, where they and army intelligence spent a week poring over classified maps of the target area. As lead navigators, their jobs were to select the necessary charts, which were copied, crated, and shipped to California to meet the crews when they boarded the *Hornet*.

Post-Raid

Along with the rest of his crew, Tom had to bail out in a severe storm, but he landed safely since his chute caught the springy tops of some bamboo trees, and he settled softly to earth. Tom describes his experience of bailing out over China in C. V. Glines's *The Doolittle Raid*: "After fifteen and a half hours in the air our motors gave the sputtering sound we had long been waiting for. The bottom hatch was opened and one by one we eased down through the black hole into nothing. Jumping at night and in a storm is an experience one will never forget. There were times during that descent from ten thousand feet when I thought I had missed the earth. The wind currents at the time must have been violent because I remember just being able to see my chute. It would be level with me and sort of fold up. Then it would swing up over my head, fill up, and come down on the other side, once again spilling its air. However, it hung up on the tops of some bamboo trees and I was lowered to earth with the greatest of ease."

Griffin was quickly sent back to the States and was assigned to B-26s in July 1942. He was sent to North Africa to fight against Rommel's forces, where he also participated in skip-bombing attacks on German shipping in the Mediterranean. His extra duty was to go forward in the plane and man a .50-caliber machine gun and sweep the decks of the freighters they were bombing. His plane was shot down on July 4, 1943, while bombing airfields in Sicily. At age twenty-six—just one week shy of his twenty-seventh birthday— he was captured by the Germans and remained a prisoner of war for twenty-two months: nineteen months in Stalag Luft III and three months in Moosburg, near Bavaria. (Stalag Luft III was a German air force POW camp that housed captured air force personnel—made famous later by *The Great Escape* movie, which was filmed in 1963.) Tom was liberated in April 1945 by some of Gen. Patton's forces, and he retired as a major in that same year.

After the war, Griffin moved to Cincinnati, where he opened an accounting business in 1949, which he ran for over thirty years until his retirement in 1982. He and his wife, Esther, were married for sixty years until her death in December 2005. Tom and Esther had two children—John, who taught for many years at Murray State University in Kentucky, and Gary, who has had a career in music and travels with his band. Maj. Griffin died on February 26,

2013, in a veterans' hospital in Ft. Thomas, Kentucky, at age ninety-six. He was buried in the Hillside Chapel in Cincinnati, Ohio.

WAYNE MAX BISSELL
Bombardier

Pre-Raid
Little information has been found about Sgt. Bissell's life. He was born October 22, 1921, in Walker, Minnesota. His family moved out west and he graduated from Vancouver High School in Washington in 1939. He was a science major and played "B" football and intramural sports. He enlisted in the army on September 14, 1939, and completed bombardier training.

Post-Raid
Shortly after bailing out, Wayne was captured by Chinese bandits. However, he seized an opportunity to just run away, so he escaped from his captors and rejoined his crew members a couple of days after the Raid. Wayne became a pilot later in July 1943 and won awards for missions in the southwest Pacific. He separated from the service in July 1945, and his highest rank was first lieutenant. He was married to Bonnie Ghormley in Vancouver in March 1948. They had five children: Nancy, Barbara, Bruce, Eric, and Mark. Wayne and Bonnie divorced in 1954. Wayne died January 9, 1997, in a Vancouver nursing home at the age of seventy-five. He was buried at the Willamette National Cemetery in Portland, Oregon.

ELDRED VON SCOTT
Flight Engineer/Gunner

Pre-Raid
"Scotty" Von Scott was born September 29, 1907, in Atlanta, Georgia. He completed three years at Union High School in Phoenix, Arizona, then enlisted in the army infantry on September 9, 1924, but soon transferred into the air corps and graduated from mechanics school.

Post-Raid

After escaping from China and returning to the States, Eldred served in England and France from February 1944 until February 1945. He was commissioned as a second lieutenant in April 1943 and served as a maintenance officer in various stateside assignments and in Korea.

Scotty and wife, Merci, had three children: Doug, Mary, and Monica. He retired from the military in September 1959 as a lieutenant colonel after twenty-nine years of service, and then he worked as a field operations analyst for North American Aviation. Col. Scott died July 31, 1978, in Anaheim, California. He was cremated, and his ashes were scattered in the Pacific. Merci died October 23, 1996, following complications from a stroke.

Lt. Horace "Sally" Crouch, Lt. Richard Joyce, S.Sgt. George Larkin Jr., Lt. Royden Stork, S.Sgt. Edwin Horton Jr.

Crew No. 10

```
Pilot........................Lt. Richard O. Joyce
Copilot......................Lt. J. Royden Stork
Navigator/Bombardier.........Lt. Horace E. Crouch
Flight Engineer........S.Sgt. George E. Larkin Jr.
Gunner................S.Sgt. Edwin W. Horton Jr.
```

RICHARD OUTCALT JOYCE
Pilot

Pre-Raid

Dick was born September 28, 1919, in Lincoln, Nebraska. He graduated from Lincoln High School in 1937 and earned a degree in business administration from the University of Nebraska in 1940. He joined the army air corps on July 26, 1940, at Omaha, Nebraska. He completed primary flying training at Glendale, California, basic flying training at Randolph Field, Texas, and advanced flying training at Kelly Field, Texas, where he was commissioned a second lieutenant in March 1941. His first assignment was to the 89th Reconnaissance Squadron at McChord Field, Washington.

Post-Raid

Following his escape from China at age twenty-two, Dick remained in the China-Burma-India theater until December 1942; he had completed twenty-four missions. He held various stateside assignments until relieved from active duty on March 10, 1946, as a lieutenant colonel. By 1945, Dick had participated in thirty-eight bomber and fighter missions. He spent the final days in the military in the States, training crews for B-25s and B-26s. His first wife was Eloise, who passed away in 2009, and his second wife was Dru, who passed away in 1989. Dick had five children (Christine, Robert, Scott, Michael, and Todd) and two stepchildren (Jill Furry and Barry Dunhaver). Following World War II, Dick returned to Lincoln, where he helped run Henkle & Joyce Wholesale Hardware Company (founded in 1900 by his father). Dick became president and served in that position until his death in 1983. Dick remained an active pilot after the war, owning a Cessna 182 and a pair of Cessna 310 light twins. He was active in community affairs, including service as a member of the Lincoln Airport Authority for nearly twenty-five years, serving several years as its chairman. He was inducted posthumously into the Nebraska Aviation Hall of Fame in 1997 along with fellow Raider Donald Fitzmaurice. Dick died February 13, 1983, in Lincoln at age sixty-three and was buried at the Wyuka Cemetery in Lincoln, Nebraska.

J. ROYDEN STORK
Copilot

Pre-Raid

Roy was born December 11, 1916, in Frost, Minnesota, but grew up in San Diego. He graduated from San Diego High School in 1933 and attended San

Diego State College for two and a half years of premed training until his schooling was interrupted by the war. He left college and joined the aviation cadet program in May 1940. He was commissioned a second lieutenant and awarded pilot wings in July 1941. His first assignment was as a B-25 pilot with the 17th Bomb Group at McChord Field, Washington, and then at Pendleton Field, Oregon, until he was selected for the Raid in February 1942.

Post-Raid

In an interview with the *Los Angeles Times* shortly after the Raid, Lt. Stork recalled bailing out with candy bars and cigarettes stuffed into his pockets. "Those bars were flung in every direction, my parachute gave such a flip," he said. "It was pouring rain, and in no time my chute was soaked with water, and I was falling very fast. I must have been knocked unconscious as I don't remember anything until I found myself lying against a tree. I lay in the rain until morning before starting out."

After the Raid, Stork was retained in India as a B-24 pilot for sixteen months—flying over the "Hump." However, Roy and other surviving Raiders were soon removed from combat flying when it was learned that the Japanese had placed a $5,000 bounty on each of their heads. Upon his return to the States, he was assigned to foreign equipment evaluation duties, and then as a pilot ferrying aircraft for the Air Transport Command. He was released from active duty in January 1946 as a captain. His two choices of employment at that time were with an oil company in New York or with 20th Century Fox as an apprentice makeup artist. The prospect of cold eastern winters helped make up his mind on the movie job!

Somewhere in the late 1940s, he met Kay Adelle—a contract dancer and stand-in and double for Gene Tierney. They dated for a long time and were married in 1957 in Malibu, California. He and Kay never had any children, but they were asked about that with the irony of having the name of "Stork." Their favorite retort was "No, we don't have the disease—we're the carriers!" Roy had a full career as a Hollywood makeup artist, working both television and movies. His best-known work was with the TV series *The Beverly Hillbillies*, and he maintained a special friendship with the show's star, Buddy Ebsen. Roy also worked on the feature film *Twelve O'Clock High* in 1949, starring Gregory Peck.

Roy and Kay had an especially happy and active time at the Raiders' sixtieth reunion in 2002 in South Carolina. However, a week after attending that event, Roy suffered a massive coronary and died a week later on May 2, 2002, in Los Angeles at age eighty-five. He was cremated, with ashes scattered in his favorite garden. In October of that same year, Kay was diagnosed with an inoperable brain tumor. Her condition rapidly deteriorated, and she died December 15, 2002. They had been married forty-four years.

HORACE ELLIS CROUCH
Navigator/Bombardier

Pre-Raid

"Sally" Crouch was born October 29, 1918, in Columbia, South Carolina. He graduated from Columbia High School in 1936 and graduated from the Citadel in 1940 with a bachelor's degree in civil engineering. Horace told Todd Joyce that he got the nickname "Sally" when he was in a YMCA boys' camp and another boy had read a book called *Sally Crouch's Cozy Home Hotel*, so he started calling Horace "Sally." Another story that has circulated is that Crouch earned the nickname "Sally" as a boy because of his reputation for being fastidious. His friends teased him with the name, and the nickname stuck. As an adult, he was neat, meticulous, and a perfectionist—qualities that served him well both in the military and after the war as a mathematics teacher. He served in the South Carolina National Guard from 1937 to 1940 and then accepted a commission as a second lieutenant on July 11, 1940. He attended bombardier, navigator, and radar training and became "triple-rated." He was a flying cadet in the first US Army Air Corps navigator school at Barksdale AFB. Early in his military career, he flew in the first coastal patrol of World War II off the Oregon and Washington coasts.

Post-Raid

After the Raid, Sally remained in the China-India-Burma theater until June 1943. He flew missions with the American Volunteer Group (the Flying Tigers) in China as a member of the 11th Bomb Squadron. He was deputy state director of selective service in South Carolina during 1948–49—just prior to the Korean War. He applied for tactical duty and became wing training officer of the 307th SAC Bomb Wing on Okinawa. He retired from the Air Force in April 1962 as a lieutenant colonel and started a civilian career in education as a classroom teacher of mathematics and drafting in several high schools. He retired from teaching in 1982.

Sally's wife, Mary Epting Crouch, died June 5, 2001 in Columbia, South Carolina. They had a daughter, Marcia, and a son, Martin. Sally died December 21, 2005, at age eighty-seven in Columbia, with burial in Greenlawn Memorial Park, Columbia.

GEORGE ELMER LARKIN JR.
Flight Engineer

Pre-Raid
George was born November 26, 1918, in New Haven, Kentucky. He graduated from New Haven High School and entered the army on November 27, 1939, at Ft. Knox, Kentucky. He graduated from airplane mechanics school and was assigned to the 89th Reconnaissance Squadron, McChord Field, Washington. Both Larkin and fellow crewmate Horton were qualified both as engineer and gunner, but on the Doolittle mission, Larkin took the role of engineer.

Post-Raid
Along with other members of his crew, George was retained in the China-Burma-India theater after the Raid. Larkin kept a personal diary of the Raid—a small, green book in which he wrote of the bombing and his subsequent escape through China. It was autographed both in English and Chinese by Madame Chiang Kai-Shek, wife of the Nationalist Chinese leader, whom he met in China. The diary lay forgotten in a trunk in his sister's home in Louisville for over forty years.

Larkin was killed in action on October 18, 1942, in a plane crash near Assam, India, while assigned to the 11th Bomb Squadron and on detached service with the 26th Fighter Squadron. This was the same crash that took the life of Raider Bob Gray, who was the pilot. The crash was just six months after the Raid—Larkin was twenty-four years old. He was first buried in the US Military Cemetery at Barrackpore, India, and later was moved to the National Memorial Cemetery of the Pacific in Punchbowl Crater, Honolulu, Hawaii.

EDWIN WESTON HORTON JR.
Gunner

Pre-Raid
Ed was born March 28, 1916, in North Eastham, Massachusetts. He attended a one-room schoolhouse in North Eastham for eight years and graduated from high school in 1934 before entering the army in September 1935 at Providence, Rhode Island. Ed served overseas with field artillery at Schofield Barracks, Hawaii, from 1935 to 1938, when he reenlisted and was assigned to the 95th Bomb Squadron at March Field, California. He completed gun turret maintenance, aircraft armorer, and aircraft mechanics schools. Both Larkin and Horton were qualified both as engineer and gunner, but on the Doolittle mission, Horton took the role of gunner.

Post-Raid

After bailing out over China, Ed landed on a mountainside and met a teacher who took him to a school and used a Chinese-English dictionary to translate. The crew was reunited in a nearby village and taken by train, bus, automobile, and plane across China and to Calcutta, India. Horton stayed in the China-Burma-India theater for another year in the 11th Bomb Squadron as an armament chief on B-25s until June 1943. He went home in 1943 on the same plane with Sally Crouch and continued in the air force until he retired in 1960. He held various stateside assignments in Oklahoma and Florida and served overseas at Wheelus Field, Tripoli, Libya. After retirement in 1960 as a master sergeant with twenty-five years of distinguished service, he worked at the newly constructed climatic lab at Eglin AFB, Florida.

Ed and his wife, Monta, had four children: Danny G. (born in 1945), Karen Elaine (1948), William R. (1952), and Katherine Ann (1955). Monta died March 22, 2005, at their home in Florida, and Sgt. Horton died November 26, 2008, in Ft. Walton Beach, Florida, from injuries suffered in a September automobile accident. He was buried with full military honors at Beal Memorial Cemetery in Ft. Walton Beach.

Lt. Frank Kappeler, Capt. Ross Greening, S.Sgt. William Birch, Lt. Kenneth Reddy, Sgt. Melvin Gardner

Crew No. 11

Pilot.........................Capt. Ross Greening
Copilot......................Lt. Kenneth E. Reddy
Navigator......................Lt. Frank Kappeler
Bombardier.................S.Sgt. William L. Birch
Flight Engineer/Gunner......Sgt. Melvin J. Gardner

CHARLES ROSS GREENING
Pilot

Pre-Raid

Ross was born November 12, 1914, in Carroll, Iowa. He graduated from Lincoln High School in Tacoma, Washington, and entered Washington State College in the fall of 1932. As Ross and his sister Shirley were attending Washington State College, Shirley introduced him to his future wife—Dorothy "Dot" Watson. He graduated in June 1936 with a bachelor's degree in fine arts and a commission as a second lieutenant in the army. He entered active duty at Ft. Lewis in Washington shortly after graduation and volunteered for flight training. He graduated from advanced flying school at Kelly Field, Texas, in June 1937. He served at bases in Louisiana and California before joining the 17th Bomb Group at Pendleton, Oregon, in June 1940. While stationed at Barksdale Air Base in Louisiana, he trekked back to Olympia, Washington, to marry his fiancée, Dot.

After being selected for the Raid, he designed and built the now-famous "twenty-cent bomb sight" that was successfully used on the mission to replace the secret Norden bombsight. The B-25s assigned to the Raid came equipped with the Norden bombsight, which was designed for use primarily at 4,000 feet or higher. The Japan raid was planned for much-lower altitudes, so the Norden was not a good choice. In addition, the Nordens were quite expensive and top secret, so it was not a good idea to risk one or more of them falling into Japanese hands. Ross got together with Sgt. Edwin Bain, his assistant technician, and they designed a simple and crude bombsight made out of scrap aluminum. It worked just fine for low-altitude bombing, so Doolittle made the decision to replace all the Nordens with this cheap but effective substitute.

Ross's B-25 was named the "*Hari Kari-er*," and his flight of three bombers was scheduled to strike Yokohama and the Kosukan naval yard at the western side of Tokyo Bay but instead had to attack alternate targets.

Post-Raid

Ross and his crew had to bail out in the dark over China—about 200 miles inland from the coast. The plane crashed in a mountainous area on the border of Zhejiang and Anhui Provinces. After escaping from China, Ross was assigned for more training and then flew B-26 bombers in the North African campaign. He flew on many raids over Italy and was shot down over Mt. Vesuvius on July 17, 1943. He was badly injured and was captured by the Germans. They sent him and other prisoners by train to a POW camp, but when the train was attacked by Allied bombers, Ross and several buddies escaped, hiding out for more than six months in the mountains of northern

Italy—sometimes living in caves. Unfortunately, he was captured a second time and spent most of the remainder of the war in the Stalag Luft I POW camp near Barth, Germany. While in prison, he honed his portrait artistry, doing portraits of the prison commandant and guards to earn extra food supplies that he could share with his fellow prisoners. He also interviewed hundreds of his fellow pilots and painted scenes depicting experiences that led to their capture. He promised his POW friends that if he survived and was able to keep his sketches, he would have them published in book form and give them each a copy. This ultimately became his book *Not as Briefed: From the Doolittle Raid to a German Stalag*. Near the war's end, Ross, the American commander of the camp, and his mates took over the camp before it could be overrun by Russian soldiers. In *Not as Briefed*, Ross describes the strange transition from German captivity to freedom in a Russian-liberated environment. Most of the German prison staff sneaked away during the night from the oncoming Russian army, leaving the inmates in control of the prison. "Maj. K. H. Steinhower, the German commandant of North 1 Compound, remained in the camp. Over the months he had fully cooperated with us within the limits of his authority, as long as he wasn't betraying his own people. He was a good guy and not a rabid Nazi, but quite a good soldier in my estimation. Shortly before the Russians arrived, Steinhower walked into my barracks, surrendered his pistol and sword, and gave me his camera as a personal gift. After saluting me smartly and saying he'd surrender to the American camp commander, he did an about face to leave the room. I pulled the gun out of its holster and put it in his back, saying, 'Major Steinhower, you are now my prisoner,' which I'm sure is exactly what he wanted me to do. He knew how grim his fate would be if captured by the Russians. I made him change clothes and put on a prisoner's garb, and we put him to work incognito in the mess hall." Through contact with Gen. Doolittle, who was then commander of the 8th Air Force, 10,000 prisoners from the camp were flown to freedom in England in just two and a half days.

After returning to the States, Ross was instrumental in getting government approval and funding to put together a traveling POW exposition. He thought it was important to educate the public about how the POWs endured their wartime imprisonment. Ross and his POW associates had collected a wealth of prison camp paraphernalia before they left the prison camp. They boxed the stuff up in Red Cross crates and got Gen. Doolittle's help in getting the military to fly it back to the States. In addition to many artifacts of prison life, the exposition included full-size replicas of a sixteen-man prison room and a solitary confinement cell, as well as a model of an escape tunnel. The show opened in New York City in 1945 and then traveled to fourteen major cities throughout the country, finally terminating a year later in Washington, DC.

Following the POW exhibit, Ross began a Cold War air force career that included jet fighter training at Panama City, Florida; group commander of the 91st Strategic Reconnaissance Group of the Strategic Air Command at McGuire AFB and Barksdale AFB in Louisiana; and duty with the Aeronautical Chart Service. For a short time, he served with the Air Force Policy Division at the Pentagon. Ross attended the Staff College, the Senior Staff Officers' School, the Air War College, and the Strategic Intelligence School. Ross and Dot started their family by adopting son Allen Ross in July 1947, and son Charles William was born in September 1949.

Ten years after release from prison, Ross and his wife revisited Italy and located the Italian friends who had helped hide him out in the mountains. Col. Greening was then assigned as air attaché to Australia and New Zealand, where his health failed. He was returned to Walter Reed Army Hospital, where on March 29, 1957, he died of bacterial endocarditis—an infection of the inner lining of the heart. He was buried at Arlington National Cemetery. Dot died in 2002 from complications of dementia, and she was buried next to Ross.

Ross's book *Not as Briefed* had an interesting development. Ross had accumulated a significant collection of wartime memorabilia, including a diary, logbook, sketches, and letters. Before his death, he had attempted to organize the material in a book with the help of a professional author. Ross recorded many of his memories on a Dictaphone, but both he and the author died before they could complete the project, and the material lay mostly forgotten in boxes for about forty years. Then one night, Ross's niece—Karen Morgan Driscoll—rediscovered the materials and started a project to write the book. With help from Ross's widow, Dot, and other family members, Karen spent five years putting all the pieces together that resulted in the final product, which was published by Washington State University Press in 2001. The book is an excellent collection of wartime experiences and sketches.

KENNETH E. REDDY
Copilot

Pre-Raid

Ken was born June 29, 1920, in Bowie, Texas. He graduated from Bowie High School in May 1937. His hobbies were fishing and horse riding. With very little money, he went off to North Texas State Teachers College and became a member of Beta Alpha Rho fraternity. He initially started out in a preministerial course but gave it up in his sophomore year to pursue a more financially rewarding career. He graduated with a BA degree in the summer of 1940 and enlisted as a flying cadet at Ft. Worth, Texas, in November 1940. He graduated from the Stockton Advanced Flying School on July 11, 1941, and was assigned to medium bombers at Pendleton Air Base, joining the 17th Bomb Group, 34th Squadron. This was the first group to get the new B-25 bombers. Various kinds of training took him to Spokane, Pendleton, Billings, St. Louis, Dayton, Wright Field, Augusta, and San Antonio. He ended up in Portland doing coastal patrol. He was soon on his way to Columbia, South Carolina, and then on to Eglin Field in Florida for the secret training for the Raid. Ken had several serious girlfriends but was never married.

In Craig Nelson's *The First Heroes*, a nervous Ken Reddy is quoted as he waits in line to take off from the *Hornet*: "The sea was rough and the airplanes were pulling against their ropes like circus elephants against their chains. Everybody was anxious to get off when his turn came, but perhaps we all felt the same—that our chances of meeting again were very few. We were shoved off 808 miles from our target, at such an hour that we would arrive in Japan in the middle of the day, and if we had gas enough to get to our field in China, it would be pitch dark. We had no weather reports. Our refueling field in China had been bombed, and we were not certain who controlled it. Nothing was in our favor."

Post-Raid

Ken returned to the States in June 1942 and began to fly extensively throughout the country on recruitment missions, rallies for war bond sales, and morale-building trips to aircraft plants. Anxious to return to combat flying, he went to Barksdale Field in Louisiana for training in a newer and faster type of aircraft—the B-26 Marauder. On the evening of September 2, 1942, he was flying on the first leg of a long trip to return to a combat area when his aircraft flew into a severe storm near Little Rock, Arkansas. The plane crashed, and Ken was killed at the age of twenty-two. He was buried with full military honors in the Elmwood Cemetery in Bowie, Texas.

FRANK ALBERT KAPPELER
Navigator

Pre-Raid

Frank was born January 2, 1914, in San Francisco. Shortly thereafter, his family moved across the bay to Alameda, where Frank attended school and graduated from Alameda High in 1932. He attended Armstrong Junior College in Berkeley and the University of California. He then attended Polytechnic College of Engineering in Oakland, where he graduated with a bachelor's in aeronautical engineering in 1938 or 1939 (while working part-time as a stevedore for the Southern Pacific Railroad). He enrolled in the Army Air Corps Flying School, class of 40E, at Glendale, California, but washed out and went to work for Douglas Aircraft in Santa Monica for approximately one and a half years. Frank then enrolled in the first army air corps–conducted school of navigation at Barksdale Field, Louisiana. Upon graduation, he was assigned to the 34th Bomb Squadron, 17th Group, at McChord Field, Washington.

In Craig Nelson's *The First Heroes*, it's reported that on the last night before the Raiders embarked from California on their way to Japan, most of the men chose to party in San Francisco. As an exception to that, Frank chose to spend the last night playing pinochle with his mom and dad in Alameda.

Post-Raid

When Frank bailed out from his B-25, his shroud lines became twisted and he had a dizzying descent. His chute caught in some tree branches when he landed, and he had to spend a cold, wet night in his harness. At daybreak, he was able to get out of his harness and started his long walk back to safety. After escaping from China, Frank was assigned to a newly formed bomb group in Karachi, India (now Pakistan). He flew one more B-25 combat mission, bombing a Japanese airfield on the Burma Road. Six B-25s were on the mission, led by Maj. Gordon Leland. Leland's B-25 and two others ran into cloud-covered peaks in the Himalayas, and all onboard were killed, including Raiders McGurl, Gardner, and Duquette. Kappeler's crew bailed out in China. Shortly thereafter, he was sent back to the States at McDill Field in August 1942 to be the group navigator for the newly activated 323rd Bomb Group, flying Martin Marauder B-26s. He flew the southern route to England, totaling twelve combat missions as lead navigator out of England. He then became staff navigator, 99th Combat Bomb Wing. As the war progressed, he went on to France and Belgium. By VE day, he had flown fifty-three combat missions in Europe. Frank returned to the States in August 1945.

Back in the United States, Frank had assignments at Travis AFB in California and Biggs AFB in Texas, flying B-36s and B-52s. He married Betty Kuntz in May 1957, and their only child, Francia, was born in October 1958 in El Paso. Frank also had assignments at Wright-Patterson AFB, Mather AFB, Castle AFB, and Yakota AFB, and he flew twenty-six combat missions in B-29s during the Korean War. In 1961, he served as deputy commander at Minot AFB as part of the Minuteman Missile Site Activation Task Force, and he retired from the Strategic Air Command in February 1966 as a lieutenant colonel. Frank and Betty settled in the Santa Rosa area of Northern California. He spent a few years driving a school bus then got his real-estate sales license and worked as a broker for the next eighteen years.

Col. Kappeler died at age ninety-six on June 23, 2010, at his home in Santa Rosa, California. He was buried at the Calvary Catholic Cemetery in Santa Rosa.

WILLIAM LLOYD BIRCH
Bombardier

Pre-Raid

Bill was born September 7, 1917, in Calexico, California. He graduated from Kern County Union High School. He joined the army air corps in September 1939 and was trained as a bombardier. He graduated from the bombsight maintenance school at Lowry Field, Colorado. Bill became a staff sergeant by 1942 and was assigned to the 34th Bomb Squadron at Camp Pendleton, Oregon, where he was selected for the Raid in February 1942.

In C. V. Glines's *The Doolittle Raid*, Bill Birch admits that he was scared and excited about the Raid. He recalled that "The takeoff was surprisingly easy, and believe me, from my bombardier's station in the nose, I could see everything that was going on. Since the *Hornet* could swing directly into the wind, there was no drift as we started our roll. My biggest worry was that the pilot might catch the 'island' with the right wing tip as he went by. Our targets were the docks, oil refineries, and warehouses between Tokyo and Yokohama. When we arrived over the coastline, it reminded me of southern California. People on the ground waved at us. We reached Tokyo northeast of the city when we were first attacked by enemy fighters. Four of them jumped us and we ran into flak. Sgt. Gardner put two of them out of action firing from the top turret. I released my bomb load of two incendiaries and two high explosives on a large oil refinery and tank farm from about 1,200 feet. There was an immediate explosion and fire broke out. With the bombs gone, we headed out to sea at about fifty feet."

Post-Raid

After the Raid, Bill was accepted into the aviation cadet program and graduated from advanced flying school in Lubbock, Texas, in June 1943. He flew B-24s and separated from the service in 1945 after almost a year in the hospital as a result of a broken back suffered in an aircraft accident. Bill met his future wife, Barbara, in Laguna Beach, California, and they were married in 1947. They had two children—Judith Ann and Jerold. Both children died of cancer within one year of each other.

Bill worked in his father's butcher shop for a while, and during the 1950s he found work in the oil fields. He apprenticed and worked as a master machinist in the aircraft industry. His love for aviation led him to become a helicopter pilot and instructor. He started a flight school and trained many young men who eventually flew combat missions in Vietnam. While flying a charter flight in 1967, he lost an engine on takeoff and crashed, resulting in another broken back. This injury forced his retirement from flying.

Bill enjoyed reading and raising raccoons in his retirement years. His wife, Barbara, died August 7, 2006, and Bill died November 18, 2006, of cancer in Temecula, California, at age eighty-nine. He was cremated, with disposition of remains unknown.

MELVIN J. GARDNER
Flight Engineer/Gunner

Pre-Raid

Mel was born April 6, 1920, in Mesa, Arizona. He went to grade school in Linden and graduated from high school in 1938 in Snowflake, Arizona. He was raised on a ranch and was very active in the Boy Scouts. In high school, he participated in sports and was vice president of his senior class. He joined the army air corps in October 1939 at age nineteen and was assigned to March Field in California, where he became happily involved in airplane mechanics. He was transferred to Chanute Field at Rantoul, Illinois, where he attended airplane mechanics school. Mel was promoted to corporal in January 1941 in the 34th Bomb Squadron and became a crew chief at McChord Field, Washington. He wrote to his father in April 1941 that they were training him to be a flight engineer, and his squadron was transitioning into the very fast B-25s. Mel was a devout Mormon, and he continued his religious study while in the army. He was engaged to Virginia Harmon, but they never got married. Mel's last two letters home were dated April 1, 1942, while he was in San Francisco getting ready to embark on the USS *Hornet*. He advised his parents not to send any more mail until they heard from him (this was only a couple of weeks before the Raid). He tried to calm his parents' worries with the thought: "Remember—no news is good news."

Post-Raid

While on their bombing run over Japan, Mel's B-25 was attacked by four Japanese fighters. Mel saved his entire crew by shooting down two of them and scaring the other two away with his effective marksmanship. After the Raid, Mel was retained in the Indochina theater and assigned to Allahabad, India, where he met up with Lt. Greening. Greening writes: "When passing through Allahabad, I met my engineer/gunner, Sgt. Melvin Gardner. He was scheduled to embark the next morning on a bombing mission in Burma and proceed to Kunming, China. I told

Gardner that I would wire him if he were in the list to return to the States. After arriving in New Delhi, I was happy to learn that twenty-seven of us from the Doolittle outfit had orders to return to the United Sates, including Sgt. Gardner. I wired Allahabad, asking to have Gardner withdrawn from any operations so he could be sent back to the States. Unfortunately, the message was pigeonholed just a little too long. Gardner took off with a flight of B-25s that bombed Lashio, Burma. When Japanese planes attacked them over the mountains, they dove into the clouds. All but two of the B-25s crashed into the mountains. Gardner was never heard from again."

Mel was killed in action June 2, 1942—just about six weeks after the Raid. His remains were never recovered. His family placed a headstone for Mel beside his parents' graves at Reed Hatch Memorial Cemetery, Taylor, Texas. His family endured another tragedy only eight months later when Mel's brother Kenneth was killed in action during a high-altitude bombing mission over Naples, Italy, on February 7, 1943. Kenneth was serving as a tail gunner in a B-24.

Crew No. 12: *left to right:*
Lt. William Pound Jr., Lt. William Bower, T.Sgt. Waldo Bither, Lt. Thadd Blanton,
S.Sgt. Omer Duquette

Crew No. 12

Pilot..........................Lt. William M. Bower
Copilot.......................Lt. Thadd H. Blanton
Navigator................Lt. William R. Pound Jr.
Bombardier.................T.Sgt. Waldo J. Bither
Flight Engineer/Gunner.....S.Sgt. Omer A. Duquette

WILLIAM MARSH BOWER
Pilot

Pre-Raid

Bill was born February 13, 1917, in Ravenna, Ohio. He got his first airplane ride at the age of nine, sitting on his grandmother's lap, when Hugh Robbins took them for a ride in his 1926 WACO biplane (made by the Weaver Aircraft Company of Ohio.) He graduated from Ravenna High School in 1934. As a teenager, Bill joined his father's cavalry unit of the Ohio National Guard. He became a skilled horseman but soon decided that the air corps would be more to his liking. When he snuck into the 1932 air races at the Cleveland Airport, he got his first glimpse of Jimmy Doolittle and Roscoe Turner—a famous pilot, barnstormer, and air racer—and the die was cast for his devotion to aviation.

Bill tried but failed to get an appointment to West Point in 1935, so he continued college for two years at Hiram College and Kent State University in Ohio. Bill was in the Ohio National Guard—107th Cavalry—from 1936 to 1938. He got accepted to aviation cadet training and went to primary training in 1939 at Tuscaloosa, Alabama, class of 1940F. After primary training, he went to Randolph Field, and then to Kelly Field. He was commissioned a second lieutenant in October 1940 and received orders to the 37th Bomb Squadron, Lowry Field, Colorado. He flew B-18s, flew photo missions, and trained bombardiers. He almost volunteered to join the Flying Tigers, but his commanding officer blocked it. Little did he know that he would meet the Flying Tigers a few months later in China!

Bill met his future wife, Lorraine Amman, in July 1941 during a brief stay at Lowry Air Base (Denver) before training took him to the southeastern United States.

In the summer of 1941, the 37th was alerted to go to Alaska but were diverted to the 17th Bomb Group at McChord Field, Washington, and cross-trained into B-25s. Bill became the engineering officer. The 17th Bomb Group went on maneuvers in July 1941, using airfields in Mississippi, Louisiana, and Georgia to practice with their new B-25 aircraft (which replaced the B-18 Bolos they had been flying). The training lasted until the end of November. At this time, they were scheduled to return to their base in Pendleton, Oregon, by way of Los Angeles. On Pearl Harbor Day (December 7, 1941), Bill was standing on the corner of Hollywood and Vine in the Hollywood section of Los Angeles, in his uniform. A yellow convertible pulled up, and the driver told him that Pearl Harbor had been attacked. The man offered Bill a ride to the airfield, where Bill manned his new B-25 and flew north along the coast looking for Japanese submarines. Along with other members of the 37th Bomb Squadron, Bill was soon on his way to South Carolina, where he was selected for the Raid.

There has been some confusion about the nickname of Bower's B-25. Some sources erroneously said it was named the "*Fickle Finger of Fate*," but the correct name was "*Werewolf.*" The confusion seems to have been caused because fifty-two or fifty-four extra army air corps crew members were loaded on the *Hornet* along with the primary sixteen planes and their eighty crew members. The extra crew members were carried for several reasons: they provided a backup in case a primary crew member got injured or sick, they already knew the aircraft and could help with maintenance, and taking them on the *Hornet* reduced the chance of any accidental leaks about the secret mission. Lt. Harvey Hinman was one of the extra trained pilots who were taken aboard the *Hornet*. Bill Bower's son Jim told me: "Dad's plane was called the '*Werewolf*' because he wanted to fly at night under the full moon. Harvey Hinman's plane was the '*Fickle Finger of Fate.*' Harvey's plane was the last to arrive at Alameda, and Harvey went on the ship without his plane."

During the Raid, Bower and his crew bombed the city of Yokohama—a city slightly south of Tokyo on the main island of Honshu. Bower's planned target was the Yokohama dockyards. However, that area had troublesome barrage balloons around it, so Bower opted to attack his secondary target—the Ogura refinery. His plane was flying about 1,100 feet high with an airspeed of about 200 miles per hour. After hitting their main target, they released some extra bombs on some factories and warehouses west of the Ogura refinery.

Post-Raid

On their escape flight to reach China, they flew over a Japanese weather boat, which they strafed and sank with their nose gun. Bower and his crew parachuted out of their B-25 over China during the night, which was his first jump from an airplane. Friendly Chinese villagers took them in. Bower and his crew joined up with Joyce's crew from the Raid's aircraft No. 10. It wasn't until about one month later that Bill's mother, Kathryn, was informed by Lt. Col. Doolittle that Bill survived the attack. After escaping through China, he soon returned to the States and was assigned to the 310th Bomber Group. This group was temporarily stationed at the Lexington County Airport in Walterboro, South Carolina, before being shipped out to England to help fight the Germans. Bill asked Lorraine to hurry down to Walterboro so they could be married before he shipped out. The men were staying at the Lady Lafayette Hotel, and Peggy Hinman was the only woman staying there. She was the wife of fellow pilot Harvey Hinman, who was to be Bill's best man. Unfortunately, Peggy was confined to bed because of her pregnancy, so she could not serve as maid of honor. So, Raider Travis Hoover (pilot of plane No. 2) stepped in and served as Lorraine's maid of honor. The wedding was on August 18, 1942, in the lobby of the hotel. Bill and Lorraine eventually had four children: William

Alvin in 1946, James Reed in 1949, Mary Catherine in 1954, and Melinda Ann in 1958.

Bill was assigned temporary duty in England in October 1942 before transferring to the command of Brig. Gen. Jimmy Doolittle and the formation of the 12th Air Force in Morocco in December 1942. After seven months with the 12th, he transitioned to the 15th Air Force under Gen. Ira Eaker, and finally to the 57th Bomb Wing, commanded by Brig. Gen. Robert A. Knapp. He remained with the 57th until the end of the war, whereupon he assumed command of the 310th Bomb Group as it was being transferred back to South Carolina in the fall of 1945. Bill decided to stay in the air force as a career. When stationed in Newfoundland, he pioneered arctic flights during the 1950s. He was the first pilot to land an airplane on an ice cap without skis—an astonishing feat at the time.

Bill was a graduate of the Command and Staff School at Maxwell AFB and at one time was assigned to the Directorate of Flight Safety Research, Office of Inspector General, at Norton AFB. At one time, he commanded Dobbins Air Force Base in Marietta, Georgia. In *The Doolittle Raiders*, C. V. Glines relates a story about the 1955 Raiders' reunion, which three of the Raiders would never forget. Bower, then commander of Dobbins AFB, Ed Horton, and Adam Williams were passengers on an air force C-47 en route to the reunion in Los Angeles. The plane departed Atlanta, where it had stopped for more passengers, and headed for Barksdale, Louisiana. A few minutes after takeoff, a propeller began to surge out of control. The pilot turned back toward the nearest airfield, but the overspeeding prop could not be controlled and the plane began to lose speed and altitude. The copilot told the passengers to throw all their baggage overboard to lighten the load, then quickly told them they would have to bail out when the plane kept losing altitude. Ten men bailed out, but Bower elected to stay with the plane, which managed to clear a ridge and landed at Fulton County Airport. When the crippled C-47 stopped, Bower leaped out and saw a helicopter warming up on the parking ramp. He quickly told the pilot what had happened and was soon back in the air searching for the ten men who had parachuted minutes before. All were found safe, although two were slightly injured. Undaunted, the three Raiders proceeded to the reunion, but without their luggage, which had been strewn over the countryside and was not found until after their return.

Bill retired as a colonel in 1966. He claimed that his strongest memory of the Doolittle Raiders was the opportunity to go into combat with his boyhood hero—Jimmy Doolittle. When Gen. Doolittle died in 1993, Bill was one of twenty-two Raiders present at Arlington National Cemetery for the funeral. Years before, Bower had sent an old bugle to Doolittle's granddaughter Jodi as a wedding gift, encouraging her to continue the Raider custom of blowing it "to rouse the sleepy troops." Jodi brought it to the funeral and asked Bill to sound taps with it. "I got through about three bars before I choked up," says Bower. "Jim's great-grandson Paul was standing next to me, so I handed him the bugle and he finished it."

Bill and Lorraine settled in Boulder, Colorado, for their retirement. Lorraine died on March 11, 2004, after a long illness. Bill died on January 10, 2011, at age ninety-three after suffering complications from a fall in 2009. Both Bill and Lorraine were buried in Arlington National Cemetery. The Colonel William Marsh Bower Center was opened at the Portage County Regional Airport just north of Ravenna in June 2013.

THADD HARRISON BLANTON
Copilot

Pre-Raid
Thadd was born February 25, 1919, in Archer City, Texas. He graduated from Gainesville High School in Texas in 1936 then attended Gainesville Junior College from 1937 to 1938. From 1939 to 1940, he attended Texas State Teachers College. He entered the army in November 1940 at Dallas, Texas, and completed flight training at California Aero Academy at Chino, California, in February 1941 and was commissioned a second lieutenant that same month. Thadd was stationed for a short time in early 1941 at Moffett Field, California, then at Stockton Field, California, for part of 1941, then on to Pendleton Field, Oregon, from July 1941 to February 1942, where he served as a B-25 pilot. Eglin Field was his last training location before going on the Japan raid.

Post-Raid
Thadd remained in China for two months after parachuting out of his plane. He was transferred to India from 1942 to 1943. During this time, he flew B-25 Mitchells out of Chakulia Airfield, India. The bomb squadrons there flew missions against enemy transportation in central Burma. The group bombed bridges, locomotives, railroad yards, and other targets to delay movement of supplies to the Japanese troops fighting in northern Burma. One story told about Thadd was that he escaped through enemy territory after a plane crash in Burma. However, a friend and fellow soldier in Chakulia told Thadd's son, Casey, that Thadd was flying over Burma in a three-plane triangular formation with Thadd in the leading plane. The two planes behind tried to switch places and crashed. Thadd's plane was the only one to fly back to the base—he did not walk out nor did his plane crash.

After World War II, Thadd was stationed first at Pinecastle AFB, Florida, from August 1943 to October 1946. He married Helen Weed in Ariton, Alabama, in 1946, and they had two children: Cassandra in 1947 and Thadd Jr. in 1948. During the following years, Thadd was stationed or active at Ladd Field, Alaska; Eglin AFB, Florida; Kwajalein Atoll in the Marshall Islands; Eglin AFB again; Patrick AFB, Florida; Grand Bahama Island; British West Indies; Patrick AFB again; and Clark AFB in the Philippines. He was involved in guided-missile operations from 1946 to 1954 at Eglin AFB and Patrick AFB.

Thadd retired from the air force as a lieutenant colonel in 1960 on a medical discharge, and the Blanton family moved to Winter Park, Florida. He died on September 27, 1961, in the Orlando Army Air Base Hospital. He was buried at the Fairview Cemetery in Gainesville, Texas. His wife, Helen, died on August 18, 2010, in New Smyrna Beach, Florida, where she lived with her daughter, Cassandra. Helen was buried in Ariton, Alabama.

WILLIAM ROY POUND JR.
Navigator

Pre-Raid
Bill was born May 18, 1918, in Milford, Utah. He attended Santa Monica Junior College, California, for two years, then entered the army's aviation cadet program in May 1940 at March Field, California. He was commissioned a second lieutenant and rated as navigator in June 1941. His first assignment was with the 37th Bomb Squadron of the 17th Bomb Group at Pendleton Army Airfield, Oregon. He was selected for the Doolittle mission about a year later.

Post-Raid
Bill returned to the States in June 1942 then served with the 379th Bomb Squadron of the 310th Bomb Group in England and North Africa from September 1942 to March 1944. During this time, he flew fifty-four missions. After serving on occupation duty in Germany after the war, Lt. Col. Pound served with the 1377th Air Force Base Unit at Westover AFB, Massachusetts, before leaving active duty in August 1948.

Bill and his wife, Louise, had three children: John, Terry, and Danny. At one time, Bill worked in sales with IBM in Santa Fe, New Mexico. He died July 13, 1967, and was buried at the Santa Fe National Cemetery.

WALDO J. BITHER
Bombardier

Pre-Raid

Waldo was born October 31, 1906, in Houlton, Maine. He graduated from Houlton High School and attended Ricker Classical Institute. He entered the army on January 27, 1925, and served in the coast artillery in the Philippines from 1925 to 1928. He transferred to the army air corps and completed armorer and bombardier/navigator training. From 1928 to 1942, he had various assignments at Ft. Crockett, Texas; Barksdale Field, Louisiana; Lowry Field, Colorado; and Pendleton Army Air Field, where he was trained as a B-25 bombardier and selected for the Doolittle Raid.

Post-Raid

After bombing a refinery in Yokohama and strafing a power station, he bailed out over China. Waldo had a potentially fatal event that occurred just before he had to bail out. Lt. Bower had called the crew together in the navigator's compartment to give them instructions on bailing out. As Waldo grabbed his chute and crawled backward in the darkness, the ripcord accidentally pulled out and the chute opened. He asked Bill Pound if he knew how to pack a parachute, but he shook his head. So Waldo asked Bill to hold it while he repacked it. Although Waldo had never packed one before, he had worked in the parachute shops repacking towropes. Doolittle explained later that Waldo was one of only two people in all sixteen crews who could have repacked a parachute. Can you imagine the feeling a guy would have in a plane about to crash who was unable to repack his opened chute?

Waldo returned to the States in June 1942 and completed officer training school. He served in England from 1943 until the end of the war in 1945. He stayed in the service after the war and served in Pyote AFB, Texas (1945–48); Kelly AFB, Texas (1948–52); and Japan (1953). He retired from the air force in January 1954 as a major with over twenty-eight years of service. After retirement, he worked for the Defense Materials Service of the General Services Administration in Eagle Pass, Texas, as a resident inspector. Waldo died February 25, 1988, at the age of eighty-one and was buried in the Greenwood Memorial Park in Ft. Worth, Texas. Waldo's wife, Sue, died in May of the same year. They had two children—Waldo James Jr. (born in 1937) and Linda Sue.

OMER ADELARD DUQUETTE
Flight Engineer/Gunner

Pre-Raid

Omer was born January 25, 1916, in West Warwick, Rhode Island. He attended high school for two years then entered the army on February 2, 1938, at Providence, Rhode Island. He served at Ft. Slocum, New York, and Albrook Field, Canal Zone, before joining the 37th Bomb Squadron at Pendleton, Oregon.

Post-Raid

Omer suffered a broken foot upon landing after the Raid. Fortunately, some sympathetic Chinese found him and helped him join his crew members. The Chinese made a sedan chair for him out of parachute harnesses and carried him the next day to where they met Joyce's crew. They all left there for Chuchow, where they were hidden and well treated for six days. They had to hide in caves during daylight hours because of Japanese air attacks. After about twenty Raiders gathered together, they all started out for Chunking, traveling by bus, train, boat, and eventually airplane.

Omer remained in the China-Burma-India theater after the Raid, serving as a B-25 gunner with the 11th Bomb Squadron. He was killed in action June 3, 1942, in Burma, only about six weeks after the Raid. His plane crashed into a mountain en route to Kunming, China, while returning from a bombing mission over Lashio, Burma. His remains were never recovered. Two other Raiders were also killed in the same crash—Lt. Gene McGurl and Sgt. Melvin Gardner.

Crew No. 13

Pilot........................Lt. Edgar E. McElroy
Copilot...................Lt. Richard A. Knobloch
Navigator.................Lt. Clayton J. Campbell
Bombardier...............Sgt. Robert C. Bourgeois
Flight Engineer/Gunner.......Sgt. Adam R. Williams

EDGAR E. MCELROY
Pilot

Pre-Raid

Mac was born March 24, 1912, in Ennis, Texas. He graduated from Ennis High School and attended Trinity University for three years on a football scholarship. He liked airplanes and automobiles and he worked in his dad's auto repair shop, where he was able to build his own Model-T out of junk parts. He entered the army in November 1940, completed pilot training, and was commissioned a second lieutenant in July 1941. Two days later, he married "Aggie" Gill in Reno, Nevada. His first assignment was to the 17th Bomb Group in Pendleton, Oregon. He was soon flying sea patrols looking for Japanese submarines, and then on to Columbia, South Carolina, followed by Eglin Field, Florida. After getting briefed in generalities on a "Special B-25 Project" by a living legend— Lt. Col. Doolittle—the crews worked aggressively to eliminate excess weight from their planes so they could add extra fuel tanks. They were able to extend the range of their B-25s from 1,000 to 2,500 miles. In addition, a navy pilot helped them practice short takeoffs. In his journal, Mac said:

"The shortest possible takeoff was obtained with flaps full down, stabilizer set three-fourths, tail heavy, full power against the brakes, and releasing the brakes simultaneously as the engines revved up to max power. We pulled back gradually on the stick and the airplane left the ground with the tail skid about one foot from the runway. It was a very unnatural and scary way to get airborne."

With only three weeks of special B-25 practice, Mac had to leave his pregnant wife and head for McClelland Air Base in Sacramento, California. He named his plane "*the Avenger*."

Mac commented in his journal: "After just three weeks of practice, we were on our way. This was it. It was time to go. It was the middle of March 1942, and I was thirty years old. Our orders were to fly to McClelland Air Base in Sacramento, California, on our own, at the lowest possible level. So here we went our way west, scraping the treetops at 160 miles per hour, and skimming along just fifty feet above plowed fields. We crossed North Texas and then the panhandle, scaring the dickens out of livestock, buzzing farmhouses and many a barn along the way. Over the Rocky Mountains and across the Mojave Desert dodging thunderstorms, we enjoyed the flight immensely and although tempted, I didn't do too much daredevil stuff. We didn't know it at the time, but it was good practice for what lay ahead of us."

Ronald Drez in his book *Twenty-Five Yards of War* explains that the *Hornet*'s intelligence officer—Lt. Cmdr. Stephen Jurika—had the responsibility to brief crew No. 13 on their mission. Jurika had the unique distinction of having graduated from the University of Tokyo, so he knew Japan quite well.

Their target was the Yokosuka naval base in Tokyo Bay, about 25 miles south of Yokohama. They were to hit the dock area and specifically an aircraft carrier and the drydock it was in. Mac's plane was to carry three high-explosive 500-pound bombs and one 500-pound incendiary cluster.

Post-Raid

Mac and his crew bailed out over China with minimal injuries. The crew arrived at Chuhsien (Chuchow) three days later, thanks to help from local friendly Chinese. The entire crew remained in Indochina to fly missions for more than a year. Mac flew a DC-3 "Gooney Bird" in the China-Burma-India theater for the next several months. He flew supplies over the Himalaya Mountains (the "Hump") into China. When B-25s finally arrived in India, he flew combat missions over Burma. Later in the war, he flew B-29s out of the Marianna Islands many times to bomb Japan. Mac elected to stay in the air force as a career.

Mac and wife, Aggie, had two sons—Edgar Jr. and Richard. Mac served in many operational assignments at squadron, group, and wing level, and he was rated as a command pilot. He served in Japan, Korea, the Mariana Islands, England, Germany, and Laos. He retired from the air force as a lieutenant colonel in 1962 after twenty-two years of service. He became a teacher at Mackenzie Junior High in Lubbock, Texas, and later worked for S&R Auto Supply. Mac died of a stroke at his Lubbock home on April 4, 2003, at age ninety-one. Aggie died of heart failure on April 27, 2006, and was buried next to Mac in the Dallas–Ft. Worth National Cemetery. They had been married for sixty-six years.

RICHARD AUGUST KNOBLOCH
Copilot

Pre-Raid

Dick was born May 27, 1918, in West Allis, Wisconsin (a suburb of Milwaukee). He began studies to be a veterinarian at the University of Wisconsin in Madison and joined the ROTC program there. It was at the university that he met the woman who would later become his wife—Rosemary Rice. He interrupted his studies by volunteering for military service as an aviation cadet. He entered the Spartan School of Aeronautics in 1940 in Tulsa, Oklahoma, graduating among the top five students of the class. In July 1941, he was commissioned a second lieutenant at Kelly Field, Texas. Less than a year later, he had volunteered for and was in training for the Doolittle Raid.

In *The First Heroes*, Craig Nelson describes the attitude of most of the *Hornet*'s crew: "The *Hornet*'s naval crewmembers and the Army Air Corps support staff were very cordial to the Raiders and admired them for their bravery." However, a few exceptions were not above trying to take advantage of the situation. Knobloch remembers that "There was a sergeant who liked the car that I owned . . . It was a Pontiac. He said, 'I'll give you $50 for that. You're not coming back anyway. You're not going to live. Give me that car for $50.' . . . When you are young, however, you don't think about it. You know if you are going to have 50 percent losses, you look at the other guy and say, 'You poor devil, you aren't going to make it!'"

Post-Raid

Years after the Raid, Dick reflected that the only time he felt real fear was right after he bailed out of his B-25. The shock of his parachute opening made him think the chute had hooked on the tail of the plane, which would have been his death sentence. Fortunately, he landed in a rice paddy—six inches of mud and water—probably the softest place to land. He always made a joke about landing in a rice paddy, saying that his girl (whose last name was Rice) was looking out for him that night. Dick remained in the China-Burma-India theater and completed more than fifty bombing missions against the Japanese forces before returning to the States in 1943.

Dick's daughter Sandra recently stated that Dick frequently flew in the company of the *Flying Tigers,* who provided protection on his missions. He greatly admired them. As for the Japanese pilots, Dick recalled that they were excellent fliers and courageous, "but they didn't have the machines we did." One of his missions took him to the Irrawaddy Valley, where he was detailed to bomb a bridge over the Burma railroad. The plan called for low-altitude bombing, and when the plane was at barely more than 100 feet he released delayed-action bombs, but not before one of his engines had been stopped by ground fire. With only one engine and a 9,000-foot climb to get him over the Naga hills, he remembers being very apprehensive. The British had advised him beforehand that a forced landing in the Naga hills would result in his capture by the Naga cannibals. British pilots were known to have had their heads cut off by them. "It was not a comforting thought to have only one motor," Dick reminisced. "Those headhunters worried me more than bullets ever had."

He married Rosemary Rice in Madison, Wisconsin, on August 1, 1943. They had two daughters—Sandra Kay and Lynda Ann.

After the Raid, Dick elected to stay in the air force for a career. Some of his assignments and accomplishments: (1) engineering officer and test pilot at Eglin Field, 1943; (2) returned to college in 1946, earning his bachelor's degree in agriculture at Kansas State College; (3) deputy assistant chief for materiel, Twelfth Air Force, March Field, California; (4) Royal Air Force Flying College, England, 1949; (5) deputy for materiel, Ninth Air Force, Pope AFB, North Carolina; (6) vice commander, 363rd Tactical Reconnaissance Wing, Shaw AFB, South Carolina, 1953; (7) Strategic Intelligence School and Foreign Service Institute, Washington, DC, 1955; (8) air attaché, Rome, Italy, 1956–60; (9) Industrial College of the Armed Forces, Ft. McNair, Washington, DC, 1960–61; (10) Officers' Assignment Division, Headquarters USAF, Pentagon; (11) deputy commander, USAF Military Personnel Center, Randolph AFB, Texas; (12) deputy chief of staff, personnel, at Headquarters, Pacific Air Forces, Hawaii; (13) commander, Andrews AFB, Maryland, 1968.

In *The First Heroes*, Craig Nelson relates the story where Brig. Gen. Knobloch was piloting a C-47 from the Pentagon to Colorado Springs when he mentioned to his copilot that he'd like to drop by and have a look at "our cups." Dick took the officer to the Air Force Academy Museum and in front of the display explained the Raider silver chalices and the significance of the downturned cups for those who were gone. The copilot—Lt. Col. Carroll V. Glines—was so moved by the story that when he retired from the service to begin a career as an author, five of his more than thirty books would cover the Doolittle story. For recording their memories, the airmen made him an honorary Raider and their official historian.

Dick retired in 1970 as a brigadier general. He then worked as a vice president for United Technologies in New York City and served on the board of Barclays Bank of New York. He served as chairman of the Doolittle Raiders Association and as president of the Wings Club, as trustee of the College of Aeronautics, and with various other organizations.

Nobby died August 13, 2001, in San Antonio at age eighty-three and was buried in the Ft. Sam Houston National Cemetery in San Antonio, Texas.

CLAYTON J. CAMPBELL
Navigator

Pre-Raid

Clayton was born March 14, 1917, in St. Maries, Idaho. He graduated from high school in Orofino, Idaho, in 1935. He attended the University of Idaho, graduating with a degree in architecture in June 1940. That spring, he became engaged to Mary Stevens, his college sweetheart. Upon graduation, he joined the army air corps and graduated from Pan American's second navigation class, receiving a commission as second lieutenant in June 1941. He and Mary were married June 10, 1941, in Moscow, Idaho. They started their marriage at

Ft. Lewis in Tacoma and then were transferred to Pendleton Field, Oregon, where he volunteered for the secret mission. They got to spend a month together at Ft. Walton Beach while the Raiders were receiving secret training at Eglin Field. Clayton's son John stated that on March 14, 1942, Clayton's twenty-fifth birthday, Mary informed him that she was pretty sure they were going to have a baby. On March 24, the Raiders left Florida and Clayton was overseas for fifteen months, missing the birth of his first son.

Post-Raid

After the Raid, Clayton was assigned to the Flying Tigers in China, where he served as squadron navigator with the 11th Bomb Squadron, along with eight other Raiders. While in China, he flew thirty-five bombing missions, some inflicting significant damage. On one mission, he bombed and sank a ship that contained 500 crated Japanese Zeros going to the Hong Kong assembly plant. Another destroyed the Hong Kong power plant. In 1943, he returned first to Spokane and then to Colorado Springs, where he taught navigation. After the war, he remained in the Air Force Reserve, eventually retiring as a lieutenant colonel in 1977. Following the war and while in the reserves, Clayton became a journeyman carpenter and worked in Boise building houses and later doing finish woodwork and cabinetry. In 1951, he designed and built the Boise home where he and Mary raised their five children—Clayton John Jr., born in 1942; Marjory Ann, in 1944; Elizabeth M., in 1947; Douglas, in 1949; and Gregory Dean, in 1952. Clayton's hobbies were camping, fishing, hunting, and gardening. He was very proud that each of his five children and all ten grandchildren were college graduates.

Clayton died of heart failure on November 17, 2002, at the age of eighty-five in Richland, Washington. Mary also died of heart failure in Richland on May 31, 2014, at age ninety-seven. They had been married for sixty-one years and are buried beside each other at Dry Creek Cemetery near Boise, Idaho.

ROBERT CLARK BOURGEOIS
Bombardier

Pre-Raid

Bob was born September 28, 1917, in LeCompte, Louisiana. He graduated from high school and attended Delgado Trade School in New Orleans. He entered the army in October 1939 in New Orleans and graduated from the Bombsight Maintenance School at Lowry AFB, Colorado, and completed bombardier training. His first assignment was as a B-25 bombardier and aircraft maintenance specialist with the 37th Bomb Squadron, until being selected for the Raid in February 1942.

In *The First Heroes*, Craig Nelson reports on one of Bob's on-ship experiences: "On board the *Hornet*, every airman checked his own equipment: pistol, water canteen, field rations, ammo clip, knife, parachute, gas mask, and some other items. 'Doc White was putting out whiskey,' remembered Bourgeois. 'He gave each of us two pints of rye whiskey to put on a snakebite or an infection. And if that didn't help, then just drink it.' The lectures—which the boys called 'skull practice'—continued daily, and now covered bombing runs, maintenance, guns, and medicine. They were told how the Chinese used night soil—human feces—to fertilize their rice fields, and were warned that Americans would have no immunity to its foreign microorganisms. The crews would have to take every nick and scratch seriously, as if their lives depended on it—since they would."

In Ronald Drez's interview with Bob for *Twenty-Five Yards of War*, Bob described the bombs: "The incendiary cluster was especially made. It contained 128 hexagon-shaped pellets about fifteen inches long with an explosive charge in the middle. The explosive charge dispersed these pellets and they were capable of burning through a three-quarter-inch piece of steel. Some targets, especially those over Tokyo, were very susceptible to fire. Lots of paper and wood." For the bomb run, Bob's plane climbed to 1,500 feet, and Bob opened the bomb bay doors out over Tokyo Bay. He was used to looking at 15- to 20-foot targets when he had practiced bombing in the Gulf of Mexico, and he would hit those targets "smack-dab" in the center. Now he was looking at a target so big, "a blind man couldn't miss it," he said about the carrier in drydock. The B-25 flew its target line. As it came closer and closer to the carrier, Bob had his thumb on the release. He dropped the three 500-pounders then dropped the incendiary bomb. He couldn't see the results from his position in the nose as the bomber zoomed over, but the copilot turned and watched as the bombs impacted. A huge ship-loading crane flew skyward and fell, shattering into pieces. The drydock, with aircraft carrier, shook and toppled onto its side and the incendiary bomb cluster scattered its 128 shards on the oil-storage tanks and the machine shop area, creating a roaring inferno. Bob closed the bomb doors and Lt. McElroy swung the plane to the left to head southwest toward China.

Post-Raid

Thirteen hours after they roared off the *Hornet*'s deck, the moment came that they hoped would not come. "The first time we really knew we were in trouble," Bourgeois said, "was when we actually ran out of gas. The red light came on the left engine and we kept running along until it quit. Mac [Lt. McElroy] feathered it while we still had power." The fuel gauge for the right engine showed a little fuel, so the plane flew on with only one engine. McElroy finally broke the silence: "Well, boys, we've got two chances. We can stay in here and we can all die, or we can try and get out and see what happens." No one said anything, and the plane continued along until the right engine started sputtering. McElroy ordered the hatch cover to be pulled, and the men started bailing out.

Bob went on to say in *The First Heroes*: "When I bailed out in China, I landed in a pond fertilized with human waste—a rice paddy. Oh, horrible! And cold and wet. Raining like hell, and I'm in it up to my neck. It sounds funny now, but it ain't funny out there, I can tell you. I crawled up on the side of the hill and sat there in the rain all night. Very cold."

Ronald Drez described another anecdote about Bob's first morning in China: "After spending the first night sitting in the rain and waiting for daybreak, Bob started walking until he spotted a man picking poppies. His mind raced to remember his training of how to distinguish Japanese from Chinese. 'We were told that the Chinese would smile at you if you smiled at them, but the Japanese would not.' He reached down into his trouser leg and retrieved his .45 and loaded and cocked it. 'Here I go,' he thought, 'I hope this sucker smiles.' He walked in laughing it up and the farmer laughed back. He made signs like he was hungry, and after much arm waving, the farmer made a motion to follow him. He took Bob to a small village. There were a few huts with mud floors and boards for beds; hogs lived in the rooms with the people. Bob was taken to the elders, who were boiling rice in a can. He watched as they added what looked like a whole pogy fish to the mixture—eyes and all. The sergeant was the first white man they had seen and they offered him some of their food, which Bob politely refused. 'I was hungry,' Bob said, 'but I wasn't that hungry.'"

After bailing out in China, Bob remained in the China-Burma-India theater until August 1943, where he completed sixty additional missions. After returning to the States, Sgt. Bourgeois was commissioned as an army flight officer in January 1944 and served as a bombsight maintenance officer until leaving active duty in March 1946. He reenlisted as a master sergeant in the army air corps in April 1946 and completed engine mechanic training and B-29 training. He then had aircraft maintenance assignments in Alaska; Biggs AFB, Texas; and Lake Charles AFB, Louisiana. He was hospitalized in 1959 and received a medical discharge in January 1960. Bob's second wife was Elizabeth Ponstein. Bob died November 13, 2001, at Metairie, Louisiana, at age eighty-four and was buried at Lake Lawn Cemetery, New Orleans, Louisiana.

ADAM RAY WILLIAMS
Flight Engineer/Gunner

Pre-Raid

Adam was born September 27, 1919, in Gastonia, North Carolina. He completed one year of high school then entered the army on September 1, 1938, at Charlotte, North Carolina. He served with field artillery before transferring to the air corps in 1939. He was assigned to the 37th Bomb Squadron at Barksdale Field, Louisiana.

Post-Raid

After bailing out over China, Adam remained in the China-Burma-India theater until June 1943. He was discharged on July 4, 1945, as a master sergeant. His wife's name was Mary. Adam was one of three Raiders who had a harrowing experience while traveling to a Raiders' reunion in April 1955. He, Bill Bower, and Ed Horton were traveling on an air force C-47 from Atlanta to the West Coast. A few minutes out of Atlanta, the propeller on the left engine began to surge out of control. After first throwing all the baggage and other loose items out of the plane to lighten the load, ten passengers, including Adam, had to bail out. Fortunately, the plane was able to land safely at a nearby airport, and the three Raiders continued on to the reunion, but without their baggage, which was strewn over the Georgia countryside.

Adam died November 30, 1993, and was buried at Hillside Memorial Gardens Cemetery, Plymouth, North Carolina.

Crew No. 14

```
Pilot.....................Maj. John A. Hilger
Copilot.......................Lt. Jack A. Sims
Navigator/Bombardier........Lt. James H. Macia Jr.
Engineer....................S.Sgt. Jacob Eierman
Gunner.......................S.Sgt. Edwin V. Bain
```

JOHN ALLEN HILGER
Pilot

Pre-Raid

Jack was born January 11, 1909, in Sherman, Texas. He graduated from Sherman High School in June 1926 and attended Texas A&M College, College Station, graduating with a bachelor's degree in mechanical engineering in 1932. He entered the US Army Reserve in May 1932 in Texas and was commissioned a second lieutenant in the infantry. He soon resigned his commission to enter the army air corps as a flying cadet in February 1933. He was again commissioned a second lieutenant in February 1935. Jack's first duty assignment after pilot training was at March Field, California, where he served as pilot, assistant base adjutant, and commander of the base photographic section. He was serving as commanding officer of the 89th Reconnaissance Squadron when the Tokyo Raid was planned, and he had been flying antisubmarine patrols. He was promoted to major in March 1942 and assigned as deputy commander with the Doolittle mission.

Hilger's targets in Japan were the military barracks surrounding Nagoya, an oil and gas storage area, an arsenal, and the Mitsubishi aircraft works. All of them were hit with precision.

Post-Raid

C. V. Glines's *The Doolittle Raid* quotes from Hilger's war diary: "I had a premonition then as to what was waiting for us and I was right. As we crossed the [Chinese] coast and continued inland the weather got worse with heavy driving rain and zero visibility. I passed the word for everyone to prepare to bail out and got ready myself. At 1920 [Chunking time] Macia estimated that we were over our objective in unoccupied China—Chuchow—and I gave the order to bail out. Everyone went out with no excitement. I've never been as lonesome in my life as I was when I looked back and found that I was all alone in the plane. I trimmed the plane for level flight and slid my seat back to get out. I had a little trouble getting between the armor plate but finally managed it and picked up my musette bag which the other fellows had laid out for me. I sat down on the edge of the escape hatch, leaned over and let go." All five flyers slept where they landed, not daring to venture far in the darkness. Hilger's diary continued: "I spent a horrible night last night. I awakened when the wind died down and I could hear what sounded like surf on three sides of me. That meant the other four fellows were out in the ocean. The last things I had seen on leaving the plane were two life jackets near the hatch. This thought kept me awake all night and it was not until more than an hour after daylight when the fog cleared that I discovered a beautiful flat valley below me and a tumbling mountain stream on either side, that had given me the illusion of surf. Columbus was never happier with a discovery than I was at that moment."

After the Raid, Jack remained in the China-Burma-India theater as a commander of a Chinese-American bomb group. During the last eighteen months of the war, he served on the staff of Adm. Chester A. Nimitz, commander-in-chief, Pacific Area, as special plans officer. He attended the Air War College at Maxwell AFB, Alabama, and the National War College at Ft. Leslie McNair, Virginia, and served in various operational and staff assignments. During the Korean War, Jack was commander of the 307th Bomb Wing, based in Okinawa. He served as commander of the US Air Force Group, Joint US Military Mission for Aid to Turkey in Ankara, from June 1957 to June 1959. In July 1959, Jack was assigned as chief of staff, Allied Air Forces Northern Europe (NATO) in Oslo, Norway. He then became chief of staff, Air Training Command, Randolph AFB, Texas in August 1961.

Jack and his wife, Virginia, had two children—Jean Adair and Sally Ann. He retired in August 1966 as a brigadier general and died February 3, 1982, at age seventy-three. Jack was cremated, and his ashes were scattered off the coast at Newport Beach, California.

JACK AHREN SIMS
Copilot

Pre-Raid
Jack was born February 23, 1919, in Kalamazoo, Michigan. He graduated from State High School in 1936, then graduated from Western Michigan University in 1940 with a bachelor's degree in liberal arts, and later received a master's from the University of Chicago in 1949 while in the army. Jack first learned to fly while a senior in college as part of a federally funded program to develop military pilots. He entered the army air corps in 1940 as part of the flying cadet program at Parks Air College in East St. Louis, Illinois. Following primary flight training, he moved to Randolph Field, San Antonio, Texas, for basic flight training. Next was advanced flight school at Brooks Field, San Antonio, where he was rated a pilot and commissioned a second lieutenant in July 1941. He was assigned to the 89th Reconnaissance Squadron, 17th Bomb Group, Pendleton, Oregon, then to Columbia, South Carolina, in 1942, where he volunteered for the Doolittle mission. Jack was twenty-three at the time of the Raid.

Post-Raid

After the Raid, Jack remained in India flying submarine patrol for a few months, then he returned to the States. He married Jane "Gabby" Mackey in Tampa, Florida, on July 6, 1942, with Maj. Jack Hilger as best man. In August 1942, he was assigned to a B-26 Marauder medium-bomber unit and served in North Africa, where he completed forty combat missions. He was the squadron commander of the 444th Bomb Squadron, 320th Bomb Group, attached to the US 12th Air Force under the command of his former Raider commander and now Brig. Gen. Jimmy Doolittle. In August 1943, he was promoted to major and led the first medium-bomber raid on Rome. On his fortieth and last mission to protect the Allied invasion of Salerno, Italy, he experienced an unusual chain of events that almost proved to be his undoing. His B-26 bomber was struck by enemy flak in the port engine, so he told Herb Macia (his navigator/bombardier) to jettison the four demolition bombs still residing in the bomb bay items to reduce weight, with a plan to gain enough distance to reach friendly territory and bail out. However, an inexperienced eighteen-year-old engineer-gunner on his first combat mission also tossed out his parachute, with no spare chutes on board. Upon discovering this, Jack realized he couldn't bail out and leave the kid alone in a pilotless plane, so he was forced to plan an emergency landing. As he approached the Allied base of Catania on the east coast of Sicily, the good starboard engine started to freeze up, making it almost impossible to make a regular up-wind landing. In addition, he had no hydraulics left, so they had to manually deploy the landing gear and could not confirm that the gear was locked down in landing position. As a final piece of bad luck, when he was preparing to land downwind on the side of the runway, the copilot feathered the good engine without forewarning or approval from Jack, thereby losing engine power and control. Although they had no power, no flaps, and no hydraulics, the landing gear turned out to be properly locked in place, so their bumpy crash landing did not set off the hanging bomb. After a quick debriefing in Operations, Jack visited the chaplain for a discussion and received a welcome share of "attitude-adjusting" spirits ("for medicinal purposes only"). Jack returned to the States, becoming a ferry pilot at New Castle Army Air Base, Wilmington, Delaware.

In 1946, Jack had to give up his reserve commission, but he reenlisted in the regular army with rank of first lieutenant, and he quickly rose back up through the ranks.

Jack graduated from the Air Command and Staff College (1952) and the Air War College (1957). He served in various stateside and overseas assignments, including as Far East air force liaison officer on Gen. MacArthur's staff during the Korean War; at the Chief Air Force Legislative Liaison Office in the US House of Representatives; at the US embassy in London as chief of the USAF-RAF Exchange Program; and as executive assistant to the deputy chief of staff, Programs and Resources, USAF Headquarters, Washington, DC. Jack retired as a colonel in July 1968 after twenty-eight years of service. In his military career, Jack completed four combat tours and eighty-five missions.

Jack and his first wife, Gabby, had three children—Michael in 1944, Bridget in 1946, and John in 1947. Jack and Gabby divorced in 1954, and Jack married Lee Adams in 1964. Jack and Lee had one daughter—Kimberly in 1969. For a number of years after retirement, Jack worked in commercial real estate in the Naples, Florida, area. With the help of A. B. Cook, Jack wrote *First over Japan* in 2002—his autobiography, published by Southpointe Press. Jack died June 9, 2007, in Naples, Florida, after a long illness at age eighty-eight. He was buried in the Naples Memorial Gardens Cemetery, North Naples, Florida.

JAMES HERBERT MACIA JR.
Navigator/Bombardier

Pre-Raid

"Chappie" Macia was born April 10, 1916, in Tombstone, Arizona. He graduated from Tombstone High School as class valedictorian and attended the University of Arizona on a football scholarship, studying mining engineering. His university studies were interrupted twice when he had to return to the family mining projects in southern Arizona for financial reasons. He joined the army air corps in June 1940 as a flying cadet, with primary training at the Ryan School of Aeronautics in San Diego. Much to his disappointment, he washed out of pilot school at the end of primary flight training, but he was then accepted into navigator training. He attended Pan American Airways' navigation school at Miami University, where he graduated with top academic rank and was commissioned a second lieutenant in June 1941. His first assignment was the 89th Reconnaissance Squadron of the 17th Bomb Group at Pendleton, Oregon. While stationed there, he married his college sweetheart, Mary Alice Murrell, in July 1941 in Spokane, Washington. Herb and Mary Alice had two sons—James H. III and Thomas E.—both of whom are retired army officers. In February 1942, the group was reassigned to Columbia, South Carolina, and became the nucleus for the Doolittle mission. Maj. Jack Hilger had been selected to be Doolittle's deputy, and Hilger picked Herb to be his navigator/bombardier.

Post-Raid

After the Raid, Herb was assigned to the 320th Bomb Group with several other Doolittle Raiders—Jack Hilger, Jack Sims, Chuck Ozuk, Ed Bain, and Dave Thatcher. The group flew B-26 Marauders and deployed to North Africa in 1942. The group was commanded by Doolittle and participated in combat operations in the Mediterranean, Sicily, Italy, Corsica, Sardinia, France, and Germany. He was with the group until April 1945, flying two combat tours (eighty missions) and serving as group navigator; group bombardier, group S-2; and finally group executive officer. When he returned to the States in April 1945, he was assigned to the Headquarters 2nd Air Force in Colorado Springs as the assistant deputy chief of staff for intelligence until the Japanese surrender in September 1945. He was then discharged from active duty and returned to Tucson, where he resumed mining opportunities with his father and later worked in the banking and automobile industries. With the outbreak of the Korean War, Herb was recalled to active duty in March 1951 at Davis Monthan AFB in Tucson. He attended the Intelligence Staff Officers course at the Air Force Command and Staff College at Maxwell AFB, Alabama, then was assigned to Headquarters USAFE, Wiesbaden, Germany, where he served as chief of policy and plans in A-2 (Intel). He was then stationed at the Pentagon in 1955, working on the exploitation of U-2 operations over the Soviet Union. He then held top intelligence or Security Service assignments at Barksdale AFB, Kelly Field, and Frankfurt, Germany, from 1959 to 1973. His last assignment was as chief of staff of the Air Force Security Service at Kelly Field, where he retired as colonel in 1973. Herb was the last Doolittle Raider to retire from active duty.

After air force retirement, Herb was the business manager for the Catholic Archdiocese of San Antonio until 1990. His wife, Mary Alice, died in 1999. Col. Macia died on December 20, 2009, at age ninety-three and was buried with Mary Alice in the Ft. Sam Houston National Cemetery, San Antonio, Texas.

JACOB EIERMAN
Engineer

Pre-Raid

Jacob was born February 2, 1913, in Baltimore, Maryland. He enlisted in the army in December 1935 at Baltimore and served at bases in New York, Hawaii, California, and Illinois before joining the 89th Reconnaissance Squadron at McChord Field in June 1940. Sgt. Eierman served as an aircraft maintenance technician and B-25 Mitchell flight engineer with the 89th Reconnaissance Squadron at McChord Field, Washington, and then at Pendleton Field, Oregon, from June 1940 until he was selected for the Doolittle mission in February 1942.

Post-Raid

After the Raid, Jacob returned to the States and served as a flight engineer on several bases, including Columbia, South Carolina; Mitchell Field, New York; and Westover Field, Massachusetts, until he entered officer candidate school in February 1945. After being commissioned as a second lieutenant at the San Antonio Aviation Cadet Center in June 1945, he served at Hensley Field, Texas; Erlangen AB, Germany; Eglin AFB, Florida; Japan; and Roslyn AFS, New York. He retired from service June 30, 1957, as a major. Jacob died January 16, 1994, and was buried at Arlington National Cemetery. His wife, Marion, is buried next to him in Arlington.

EDWIN VANCE BAIN
Gunner

Pre-Raid

Edwin was born September 23, 1917, in Greensboro, North Carolina. He attended Garfield High School in Los Angeles and entered the army on August 20, 1936. He graduated from radio repair and operator school at Chanute Field, Illinois. He was serving as a radio operator and aerial gunner on B-25 bombers with the 89th Reconnaissance Squadron at McChord Field, Washington, when he was selected for the Raid.

Post-Raid

After the Raid, Edwin was sent to Burma. On one combat mission, his plane crashed and he survived seventeen hours in the ocean. After returning to the States, Edwin transferred to the 320th Bomb Group at MacDill Field, Florida, in June 1942, and then he deployed with his unit to North Africa in December

1942. He was serving as a gunner on B-26 bombers when he survived another crash in North Africa in which he helped rescue four men from a burning aircraft. He was killed in action on July 19, 1943, when his plane crashed in the Tyrrhenian Sea while returning from a combat mission near Rome, Italy. He had been helping others bail out of the plane, and he waited too long to help himself. By the time twenty-five year-old Edwin could jump, the plane was too low—he died in the crash. His remains were not recovered. He was a master sergeant at the time of his death.

Crew No. 15: *left to right:*
Lt. Howard Sessler, Lt. Donald Smith, Lt. Thomas White, Lt. Griffith Williams,
Sgt. Edward Saylor

Crew No. 15

```
Pilot.....................Lt. Donald G. Smith
Copilot...................Lt. Griffith P. Williams
Navigator/Bombardier........Lt. Howard A. Sessler
Gunner/Physician..........Lt. Thomas R. White (MD)
Engineer..................Sgt. Edward J. Saylor
```

DONALD GREGORY SMITH
Pilot

Pre-Raid

Don was born January 15, 1918, in Oldham, South Dakota. He graduated from the Belle Fourche High School in South Dakota and received a bachelor's degree from the University of South Dakota in June 1940. He was commissioned as a second lieutenant in the infantry through the army's ROTC program. He then became a flying cadet in July 1940 and completed flight training as a pilot in March 1941 at Kelly Field, Texas. He married his fiancée, Marie, in June 1941, and they had one daughter—Donna Marie in 1942. His first assignment was with the 34th Bomb Squadron at Pendleton Field, Oregon, until he was selected for the Raid in February 1942. Don's B-25 was named "TNT."

In *The First Heroes*, Craig Nelson relates Don's frightening experience while sitting on the deck of the *Hornet* waiting his turn to take off: "Having the next-to-last plane to take off from the *Hornet*, Don had plenty of time to get nervous waiting his turn. He had a hair-raising moment when he gunned both engines and his bird wouldn't budge. Every instrument checked out fine, and nobody could find a reason for the problem. Would his crew be the only one to get washed out from the mission at the last moment? As Don fumed, he looked out to see one of the deckhands waving—they'd forgotten to pull the wheel chocks!"

Post-Raid

Don ditched his B-25 in the ocean near a small island near Sangchow. He and his crew safely evaded Japanese searchers along the coast by hiding in a Chinese junk. Don returned to the States after the Raid and was assigned to the 432nd Bomb Squadron at Barksdale, Louisiana. He was killed in action in western Europe as a result of injuries sustained in a B-26 crash on November 12, 1942—just seven months after the Raid. He was a captain at the time of his crash. Don was buried in the Pine Slope Cemetery at Belle Fourche, South Dakota.

GRIFFITH PAUL WILLIAMS
Copilot

Pre-Raid

"Griff" was born July 10, 1920, in Chicago, Illinois. He completed two years of college and enlisted as a flying cadet in November 1940 at Hemet, California. He was commissioned as a second lieutenant and rated as pilot in July 1941. He was assigned to the 89th Reconnaissance Squadron.

Post-Raid

Following the Raid, Griff remained in the China-Burma-India theater until July 1942. He was later assigned to the 12th Air Force in North Africa and was shot down in July 1943. He was captured and remained a prisoner of war until April 29, 1945. He retired as a major in January 1952.

Griff and his wife, Barbara, had four children—Richard, Janet, Margaret, and Rebecca. Griff died at age seventy-eight on August 14, 1998, and was buried in the Ft. Rosecrans National Cemetery, San Diego, California. Barbara died in 2013.

HOWARD ALBERT SESSLER
Navigator/Bombardier

Pre-Raid

Howard was born August 11, 1917, in Boston, Massachusetts. He graduated from Arlington High School in Arlington, Massachusetts, and entered the army air corps in December 1940 at Boston. He graduated from bombardier training and was commissioned a second lieutenant in August 1941. He then completed navigator training in December 1941. His first assignment was as a B-25 bombardier-navigator with the 34th Bomb Squadron at Pendleton Field, Oregon, until he was selected for the Raid in February 1942.

In *The First Heroes*, Craig Nelson relates Howard's attitude about the mission: "No matter how many times the military leaders warned the volunteers about how dangerous the mission would be, most couldn't help but feel devil-may-care. 'We were young, and we really didn't give a damn,' said Sessler, a twenty-four-year-old from Boston. 'When they said 'You're going to help the war effort,' all of us thought it was about time we did something. We weren't scared. Nobody knew what it was to be shot at. It was just like a sport. Like football or basketball.'"

Post-Raid

Following the Raid, Howard remained in the China-Burma-India theater until July 1942. He then served in the European theater from September 1942 until September 1943, and then in the Mediterranean theater from September 1944 until 1945 (no information was found on the intervening year). He was discharged from active duty as a major in November 1945.

After the military, Howard went to college and graduated from the University of Southern California in 1950 with a bachelor's degree in civil engineering. He became the owner and president of a heavy construction firm. Howard and his wife, Francis, had one daughter, Barbara. Howard died

February 9, 2001, in Thousand Oaks, California. He was cremated, with ashes scattered off the Los Angeles County coast.

THOMAS ROBERT WHITE
Gunner/Physician

Pre-Raid

"Doc" White was born March 29, 1909, in Haiku, Maui, Hawaii. He graduated from Redlands High School, Redlands, California, in 1927. He graduated from the California Institute of Technology with a bachelor's degree in 1931 then took postgraduate work at Harvard University and the University of Southern California. He was awarded an MD degree from Harvard Medical School in 1937 then took more postgraduate training at Johns Hopkins and interned in Baltimore and Honolulu. Doc joined the Army Air Corps in June 1941 and became a flight surgeon with the 89th Reconnaissance Squadron. When he heard about the call for volunteers for Doolittle's mission, he wired Maj. Hilger—Doolittle's deputy—and asked "to be squeezed in somewhere" on the mission. Hilger thought a physician would be a great asset on the mission, but he told Doc that the only way he could go would be as a gunner, and Doc wasn't qualified. However, Doc quickly got himself qualified as a gunner—with very high marks—and he earned himself a ride.

Post-Raid

Doc and his crew members barely escaped through Japanese lines after their plane ditched in the ocean. On their way toward Chuchow, they learned that Lt. Ted Lawson and his crew were badly injured and were headed toward a hospital in Linhai. Doc decided to detour to Linhai to see if he could help out in any way. This was a fortuitous decision, since Lawson was near death with a severely infected leg and other injuries. Doc had to perform an emergency amputation under crude conditions, which saved Lawson's life.

After the Raid, Doc took part in the initial landings in North Africa and Sicily and served in England. He was discharged as a major. After the war, he returned to private practice, specializing in obstetrics and gynecology. He opened an office in Kailua, Oahu, in 1954. He moved to Redlands, California, in 1959 and retired in Palm Springs, California, in 1963. Doc and his wife, Edith, had three children—Nelson H., Roberta K., and Florence. Doc died of pneumonia and heart disease at age eighty-three on November 29, 1992, at the Eisenhower Medical Center in Rancho Mirage, California. He was buried at the Hillside Cemetery in Redlands, California.

EDWARD JOSEPH SAYLOR
Engineer

Pre-Raid
Ed was born March 15, 1920, in Brusett, Montana. He graduated from Garfield County High School in Jordan, Montana, in 1937. After spending two years working in the western states as a logger, farmhand, and cowpuncher, he enlisted in the army on December 7, 1939, at Ft. George Wright, Spokane, Washington, and attended an air corps training school at Chanute Field, Illinois.

Post-Raid
Ed was interviewed by *YANK* newspaper about a year after the war. His comments were quoted in Stan Cohen's *Destination: Tokyo*. Ed was describing his thoughts during the bombing run over Kobe: "The skies are still empty and vacant and very clear. It's 1:43 now, and we're all at battle stations. Our pilot is Lt. Donald G. Smith of San Antonio, Texas, and he knows his business. He can throw this little old ship around like I once saw a guy throw an old Jenny around at a fair back in Montana, and he could do more things with that Jenny than a monkey can do with a coconut. Smith is sure good all right. When we started coming into Japan, he skimmed the waves so close I could almost taste the salt water from the spray in my mouth, no kidding. Our navigator-bombardier is a guy named Lt. Howard A. Sessler. He's from Boston and he's ready to go to work with his bombsight. Hirohito, you better watch out for guys named Sessler and guys from Boston. Now this will give you birds a laugh. Here we are siting up over Japan in a few hundred-thousand-bucks-worth of airplanes, and what kind of bombsight you think we got? The damned thing cost twenty cents, no kidding. Doolittle—Gen. Doolittle—he was afraid that in case any one of us got shot down, we didn't want the Japs to get hold of those Norden bombsights. So we rigged up a sight that cost twenty cents. But, brother, that sight is going to cost Emperor Hirohito and what they call the Elder Statesmen several million bucks' worth of stuff in a few minutes."

Ed continues the story a few minutes later: "We're coming in at 2,000 feet. Lt. Sessler is talking over the inter-phone in his Boston accent which always gives me a hell of a boot, it sounds so English: 'That's our baby,' the looie is saying. 'I see the target.' She's an aircraft factory, a mess of buildings down there, scattered over a block or better. There are the docks. All we got to do now is let go. Hirohito, the Yanks are coming, sprinkling it along the course. 'Let 'er go, Sess,' Smith yells to the bombardier. I felt her go when she went. The bombs, I mean. Sweet as you please that B-25 takes a sudden uplift, a little bit of a lurch, and the minute I feel it I know: Hirohito, the Yanks have arrived."

After the Raid, Ed served the remainder of the war in Europe, and he received a battlefield commission in March 1945. He served as an aircraft maintenance officer until leaving active duty in March 1946, but he continued to serve in the US Air Force Reserve. He returned to active duty in October 1947 and served as an aircraft maintenance officer at such bases as Sioux City, Iowa; Moses Lake AFB, Paine AFB, Geiger Field, and McChord Field—all in Washington; Goose AFB, Newfoundland; England; and Richards Gebaur AFB, Missouri. Ed retired from the air force as a lieutenant colonel in 1967 after twenty-eight years service, and he then worked in the real estate, home construction, and restaurant industries in Graham, Washington. Ed and his wife, Lorraine, had three children—Charlotte, Eddie, and Rod.

By the 2013 Raiders' reunion, Col. Saylor was one of only four remaining Raider survivors, so they decided to open the bottle of 1896 Hennessy Very Special cognac that Gen. Doolittle had set aside for the final survivors. Dick Cole, David Thatcher, and Ed Saylor sipped the final toast from the silver goblets with their names inscribed, although the fourth survivor—Robert Hite—was too ill to attend.

Col. Saylor died of natural causes on January 28, 2015, at an assisted living facility in Sumner, Washington, at age ninety-four. He was buried at the Tahoma National Cemetery in Kent, Washington. Ed's wife, Lorraine, died in 2011—they had been married for sixty-nine years.

Lt. George Barr, Lt. William Farrow, Cpl. Jacob DeShazer, Lt. Robert Hite, Sgt. Harold Spatz

Crew No. 16

Pilot.....................Lt. William G. Farrow
Copilot.........................Lt. Robert L. Hite
Navigator........................Lt. George Barr
Bombardier....................Cpl. Jacob DeShazer
Engineer/Gunner...............Sgt. Harold A. Spatz

WILLIAM GLOVER FARROW
Pilot

Pre-Raid

Bill was born September 24, 1918, in Darlington, South Carolina. He graduated from St. John's High School in 1935 and attended two years at the University of South Carolina. Bill's army enlistment record lists his civilian occupation as "Actor or Director or Entertainer" (it's not known if this was a joke, since George Barr's enlistment record shows the same thing). He entered the army air corps as an aviation cadet in November 1940 at Ft. Jackson, Columbia, South Carolina. He completed flight training at Kelly Field, Texas, and was commissioned as second lieutenant in July 1941. His first assignment was with the 34th Bomb Squadron at Pendleton Field, Oregon. Bill's B-25 was the last one to leave the deck of the USS *Hornet*, and it carried the name "*Bat Out of Hell*."

Post-Raid

Running low on fuel, Bill and his crew had to bail out close to the Japanese-held city of Nanchang. Within an hour, Lt. Barr had been captured, and before long all five crew members became prisoners of war. They were imprisoned and later taken to Tokyo, where they were interrogated and tortured for many weeks. Each was eventually forced to sign statements that he had committed crimes against the Japanese people. They were tried and convicted, and Farrow, Hallmark, and Spatz were sentenced to death. Wikipedia reports that the night before Lt. Farrow's execution, the Japanese gave him the opportunity to write final letters. In a letter addressed to his mother, Farrow wrote: "You have given me much, so much more to me than I have returned, but such is the Christian way. You are and always will be a real angel. Be brave and strong for my sake. I love you, Mom, from the depths of a full heart . . . don't let this get you down. Just remember God will make everything right and that I'll see you again in the hereafter. So let me implore you to keep your chin up. PS: My insurance policy is in my bag in a small tent in Columbia. Read *Thanatopsis* by Bryant if you want to know how I am taking this. My faith in God is complete, so I am unafraid."

After months of torture, Bill was executed by a Japanese firing squad on October 15, 1942, along with Dean Hallmark and Harold Spatz. They were executed at Kiangwan Cemetery near Shanghai. The Japanese cremated Bill's body. His remains were located after the war and returned to the States, where they were buried in Arlington National Cemetery. An additional memorial marker was installed in a cemetery in Darlington, South Carolina.

ROBERT LOWELL HITE
Copilot

Pre-Raid

Bob was born March 3, 1920, on a farm outside Odell, Texas. He attended grade school in Vernon, Texas, and graduated from Springlake High School in Lamb County. He attended two and a half years of college at Texas State Teachers College at Canyon. Bob became an aviation cadet on September 9, 1940, at Lubbock, Texas. He was commissioned a second lieutenant and rated as pilot in May 1941. After completing B-25 training, he was assigned to the 89th Reconnaissance Squadron at McChord Field, Washington, until selected for the Raid.

In his book *War Stories II: Heroism in the Pacific*, Oliver North published an excerpt from Bob's journal that discussed the takeoff from the *Hornet*: "Yeah, the space that we had for takeoff was from the island to the end of the flight deck, about 400 feet. So we had that much to get off of the carrier. But the secret of being able to do this was, we had about a thirty-knot wind that we were going into, a west wind. And the carrier was traveling at about close to thirty knots, so that gave us a wind across the deck of about sixty knots. This was very advantageous for what we were going to do. We used full flaps and full power on our B-25s, which was enough to lift us from the carrier. The original plan was to take off in the evening and do our bombing raid at night. That changed after they sank the Japanese patrol boat that had radioed that we were coming. So Jimmy and the commander from the *Hornet*, and Halsey with the *Enterprise* decided we better get those B-25s off the deck and on the way. Jimmy took off at 8:20 a.m. and we were the last aircraft, number sixteen, taking off at 9:20 a.m., so it took one hour to get the American B-25s off the *Hornet*. Once we were at altitude, we made meticulous use of the mixture control and our rpm to minimize the flow of gasoline through the engine. The standard B-25 engine runs on about 150 to 160 gallons an hour, but we had our B-25 running at about sixty gallons per hour. We had planned to launch within about 400 miles of our target, but we actually took off about 700 miles out."

Post-Raid

The Japanese captured Bob and all his crew members. They were interrogated and tortured in Japan for about forty-five days then were sent back to Shanghai for imprisonment. He was a POW for about forty months and then liberated by American troops on August 20, 1945. His weight had dropped from 180 to 76 pounds. After returning to the States and recovering from his injuries, Maj. Hite served with the 100th Army Air Force Base Unit at Mitchell Field, New York, until he left active duty and joined the air force reserve in September 1947.

Bob met Portia Faires Wallace at Enid, Oklahoma, in September 1946. They were married in March 1947 and ultimately had two children—Catherine Ann and Robert Wallace. After the war, Bob worked in the hotel industry but kept active in the reserves at Vance AFB, Oklahoma. During the Korean War, Bob was recalled to active duty in March 1951. He served as instructor pilot with the 3575th Pilot Training Wing at Vance AFB, Oklahoma, from March 1951 to September 1954. He then served in Morocco from September 1954 until he left active duty and returned to the reserves in November 1955. He remained in the reserves until his retirement as a lieutenant colonel in January 1969. For many years after 1955, Bob worked with Holiday Inns at various locations in Texas and Oklahoma. He retired to Camden, Arizona, and enjoyed hobbies of gardening, fishing, and golf. His wife, Portia, died in July 1999 after a marriage of fifty years. After Portia's death, Bob married Dottie Fitzhugh, the widow of Maj. William Fitzhugh, another Doolittle Raider. Lt. Col. Hite died of heart failure while battling Alzheimer's on March 29, 2015, at age ninety-five, while living in a nursing home in Nashville, Tennessee. He was buried in the Memorial Park Cemetery in Camden, Arizona.

GEORGE BARR
Navigator

Pre-Raid

George was born April 6, 1917, in New York City. He was orphaned at an early age when his father disappeared while fishing on Long Island Sound. His mother tried to support George and his sister, Grace, but was unable to do so, so George and Grace were sent to foster homes when he was only nine. George graduated from Yonkers High School. He entered the army air corps in February 1941 at Wausau, Wisconsin, and completed navigator training and was commissioned a second lieutenant at Pendleton, Oregon, on December 6, 1941. His army enlistment record listed his civilian occupation as "Actor, Director, or Entertainer" (this may have been his joke, since it was recorded that Bill Farrow did the same thing).

Post-Raid

In *The Doolittle Raid*, C. V. Glines recounts George's experience with bailing out of his plane: "George landed easily in a rice paddy up to his waist in water. Except for a slight sprain, he was unhurt. 'I wandered around in a maze of rice paddies in the dark trying to find a path. Directly in front of me was a dirt barricade with an entrance. I walked through it. Just as I did, a soldier shouted something at me and shoved a rifle in my back. My heart stood still. Was he Japanese or Chinese? He didn't shoot me but prodded me to a dugout where he woke up some other soldiers sleeping on the ground. They searched me and then tied my hands in front and my elbows behind me and marched me into a nearby town. I was still hoping they were Chinese just doing their duty but when we got to the town I was brought into a room where there were about ten to fifteen Japanese officers in full military dress sitting around a table overloaded with wines, whiskies, cigarettes, and delicacies. Needless to say, they were delighted with their captive. I was a rare prize. They immediately interrogated me through an interpreter. After refusing the food and drink and giving them only my name, rank, and serial number, I was directed to a room where I could sleep.'" The Japanese captured George and all his crew members, and George was held prisoner of war from April 1942 until August 1945.

George was the victim of a disastrous experience at the hands of the American military. From the time of his release from Japanese custody, he got caught up in a series of medical administrative foul-ups. Jimmy Doolittle relates the story in his book *I Could Never Be So Lucky Again*. George had been too weak and mentally unstable to immediately travel home, so he was kept under medical care in a Peking hotel. When he improved a little, he was transferred under restraint as a mental patient to Kunming, then to Calcutta, and then back to Kunming. He was eventually flown back to the States with medical escorts. He ended up in a military hospital with no uniform, no records, and no money. He became overwhelmed and desperate and tried to hang himself. Nobody believed his story about being on the Doolittle Raid. The Army shipped him by train in straightjacket to Schick General Hospital in Clinton, Iowa, where he was treated as a mental patient. Fortunately, some family members found out where he was, and they contacted Doolittle (who was now a general) and Jimmy came to his rescue. Jimmy immediately flew to Clinton and learned the horror story of how Bill was being treated. In a state of extreme anger, Jimmy immediately went to the hospital commander's office and unloaded his fury. As a result, George was quickly outfitted in a new uniform, was given a check for over $7,000 in back pay, got orders for a promotion to first lieutenant, and was soon seen by a psychiatrist and started his slow road to recovery.

He was retired from the army for physical disability in September 1947. George met Marcine Anderson in Ashland, Wisconsin, in December 1946, when he was recuperating from his POW deprivations. They were married on December 14, 1946, and settled in Ashland for many years. They had four children—Christy Ann, Mary Jo, Jeffrey, and Linda. George's final assignment was assistant operations officer at Mitchell Field in New York, from where he was medically retired in September 1947.

George earned a bachelor's degree from Northland College in Ashland, and a master's degree from Columbia University, New York. He was employed as a management analyst for the army. He first worked for the US Army Corps of Engineers and then transferred to the US Weapons Command at Rock Island Arsenal, where he remained until his untimely death on July 12, 1967. He died at age fifty while attending a course at Wright Patterson AFB; he was buried in Mount Hope Lutheran Cemetery in Ashland, Wisconsin. His wife, Marcine, died in March 2007.

JACOB DANIEL DESHAZER
Bombardier

Pre-Raid

Jake was born November 15, 1912, in West Stayton, Oregon, to a wheat-farming family. He graduated from Madras High School in Madras, Oregon, in 1931 and enlisted in the army in February 1940 at Ft. McDowell, California. He attended bombardier and airplane mechanics schools.

Early in Oliver North's *War Stories II*, Jake comments on the decision to launch the Raiders: "The announcement came, 'Army personnel, get your airplanes ready; in ten hours will be takeoff.' And just after they said that, the fog lifted up and we saw a Japanese ship. We could all see it. And one of our ships turned and shot into that Japanese ship and I could see it sinking. One end was up, the other end headed for the bottom of the sea. Right after that happened, they made the announcement: 'Army personnel, man your airplanes, take off immediately.'"

Post-Raid

Jake and his crew members all were captured by the Japanese, and Jake spent forty months as a prisoner of war. Jake had a life-changing spiritual experience in prison as he read and memorized large portions of the Bible. After his release from prison, he decided to become a missionary and to return to Japan to build churches and preach the gospel. He studied biblical literature and theology at the Seattle Pacific College and Asbury Theological Seminary, eventually earning a master of divinity degree. He spent more than three decades as a Free Methodist missionary, with much of that time in Japan. Both Jake and his wife, Florence, became fluent in Japanese, and she helped him establish twenty-three churches in Japan. Jake and Florence had five children— Paul, John, Mark, Carol Aiko, and Ruth.

Perhaps Jake's most dramatic conversion that received international attention was when Jake's life touched that of Commander Mitsuo Fuchida, the leader of the Japanese attack on Pearl Harbor. Fuchida received some literature one day from Jake, which put him on the path to reading the Bible and converting to Christianity. Fuchida also became an evangelist in Japan and the Orient, and he frequently preached with Jake at rallies, conventions, and church services.

Jake retired from missionary work in Japan and returned to the States in 1977, whereupon he did public speaking throughout the United States and Canada until being named assistant pastor at the Free Methodist Church of Salem, Oregon. A book was written about his life by C. Hoyt Watson, titled *DeShazer* (first published in 1991), and another book was coauthored by his daughter Carol Aiko, titled *Return of the Raider*, published in 2010. Jake died March 15, 2008, at age ninety-five in his home in Salem, Oregon. He was buried in Restlawn Memory Gardens, West Salem, Oregon.

HAROLD A. SPATZ
Engineer/Gunner

Pre-Raid

"Skinny" Spatz was born July 14, 1921, in Lebo, Kansas. He graduated from Lebo High School in June 1939, and he and two buddies entered the army in November 1939 at Ft. Riley, Kansas. He received training as an aircraft mechanic at Glendale, California, from September 1940 to March 1941. Harold became a member of the 377th Bomb Squadron, 309th Bomber Group.

Post-Raid

The Japanese captured Harold and all his crew members. About six months after the Raid, Harold and Bill Farrow and Dean Hallmark were executed by a Japanese firing squad on October 15, 1942, near Shanghai. Before being executed and cremated, these three soldiers were told to write letters to their families. C. V. Glines reports in *The Doolittle Raiders* that the Japanese used Caesar Luis dos Remedios as the interpreter between the Japanese and the Raiders. Remedios was half Portuguese and half Japanese and had been sentenced to seven years imprisonment for spying. He was fluent both in Chinese and English. Harold wrote this to his dad: "I want you to know that I have died fighting for my country like a soldier. My clothes are all I have of value. I give them to you. And Dad, I want you to know I love you. May God bless you." Unfortunately, Harold's family did not learn of his fate until the war had ended. His remains were recovered and reburied in the National Memorial Cemetery of the Pacific in Honolulu, Hawaii. A tombstone is also in place at the Lebo Cemetery. After the war, Harold's family received the Purple Heart, the Prisoner of War Medal, the Distinguished Flying Cross, and the Aerial Gunner Badge that had been awarded to Harold.

Harold's death had a dramatic impact on the community of Lebo, Kansas. In 1997, an engraved memorial stone placed in the center of Lebo was gifted by Harold's sister, Reba Jean Spatz Barnett, honoring Harold and five Lebo service men who died for their country in World War II. On May 20, 2000, the Department of the Air Force at McConnell Air Force Base in Wichita, Kansas, dedicated an enlisted dormitory as "Spatz Hall" in Harold's honor. In November 2003 Harold's sister-in-law, Caroline Busboom Spatz, donated land for the "Harold A. 'Skinny' Spatz Memorial Park."

Carolyn Spatz Davidson is a cousin to Harold, and she had an interesting story to tell about the effect of Harold's wartime experience on the younger generation. Carolyn's twenty-two-year-old granddaughter is Kaitlyn Davidson, and she is a student at the University of Hawaii. Carolyn asked her granddaughter in March 2014 to go to the National Memorial Cemetery of the Pacific in Honolulu and locate Harold's grave. Kaitlyn did so with her friend Aaron and shared these thoughts with her grandmother: "The National Memorial Cemetery of the Pacific was very beautiful, peaceful and quiet there. Once Aaron and I found Harold Spatz's gravestone, we sat next to it for half an hour talking about him and just couldn't believe what he did and were blown away by this whole thing! Aaron wanted me to tell you that he loved this idea of doing this and that he thanks you. He was very touched and emotional, while I was too, when we were sitting around Harold's grave reading the story on what happened to him during the war. We couldn't believe that he was only twenty-two years old when he died, which had us thinking more on how great he was and how much he accomplished before he died at that age! Aaron said that even though he is not related or even knew or heard about him, he felt like he knew Harold already. It was an amazing experience. Aaron helped me pick out some flowers to put on his grave. It was definitely one of the best adventures Aaron and I have had."

Epilogue

Dick Cole is the oldest surviving Raider, and his longevity has been amazing. As I was nearing the end of writing this book around mid-2017, I learned from Dick's son Rich that Dick had taken a bad fall at age 101 that broke his arm and hip. The doctors felt he was weakening, so they admitted him into hospice care. Many months went by without any further report on his condition. I recently contacted Rich to check on his Dad's status. I was pleasantly surprised to learn that Dick had recovered from his injuries and was released from hospice, and was back to travelling with his daughter! His family planned to have a nice quiet 102nd birthday for him last September. Instead, a crowd of about 180 people attended, along with a flyby of multiple aircraft. His family decided they had better start planning for his 103rd birthday party in 2018!

Unfortunately, Ellen Lawson passed away in 2009 before this book was finished. Her dedication to the Raiders' history was supported by a superb memory which significantly supplemented her Raider memorabilia and ephemera collection. Her large living room looked more like an Air Force museum than a family home. The walls were covered with rare and unique artwork, documents, curios and photos of the Raiders and Chinese officials.

The last Raiders' Reunion was held in April 2013 at Ft. Walton Beach, Florida, near Eglin AFB where it all started. There were only four surviving Raiders, but only Cole, Saylor, and Thatcher could attend—Hite was too ill to travel. It was decided to open the rare 1896 bottle of cognac and have the final toast at a special event to be held in November 2013 at the Air Force Museum at Wright-Patterson AFB, Dayton, Ohio. This event signaled the end of a famous chapter in military aviation history. Dick Cole will close the final page.

Bibliography

Cohen, Stan. *Destination: Tokyo*. Missoula, MT: Pictorial Histories Publishing, 2004.

Doolittle, Gen. James H., and Carroll V. Glines. *I Could Never Be So Lucky Again*. Atglen, PA: Schiffer, 1994.

Drez, Ronald J. *Twenty-Five Yards of War: The Extraordinary Courage of Ordinary Men in World War II*. New York: Hyperion, 2001.

Emmens, Lt. Col. Robert G. *Guests of the Kremlin*. New York: Ishi Press International, 2007.

Glines, Carroll V. *The Doolittle Raid: America's Daring First Strike against Japan*. West Chester, PA: Schiffer, 1991.

Glines, Carroll V. *Master of the Calculated Risk*. Missoula, MT: Pictorial Histories Publishing, 2002.

Glines, Carroll V. *Four Came Home*. Missoula, MT: Pictorial Histories Publishing, 2005.

Goldstein, Donald M., and Carol Aiko DeShazer Dixon. *Return of the Raider: A Doolittle Raider's Story of War & Forgiveness*. Lake Mary, FL: Creation House, 2010.

Greening, Col. C. Ross. *Not as Briefed: From the Doolittle Raid to a German Stalag*. Pullman: Washington State University Press, 2001.

Hoppes, Jonna Doolittle. *Calculated Risk: The Extraordinary Life of Jimmy Doolittle—Aviation Pioneer and World War II Hero*. Santa Monica, CA: Santa Monica Press, 2005.

John, Finn J. D. "Oregon's Doolittle Raiders Made History in Startling Ways." May 3, 2015. www.offbeatoregon.com.

Joyce, Todd. "The Official Website of the Doolittle Tokyo Raiders." Last modified November 4, 2013. www.doolittleraider.com.

Lawson, Capt. Ted. *Thirty Seconds over Tokyo*. Washington, DC: Brassey's, 2003.

Nelson, Craig. *The First Heroes: The Extraordinary Story of the Doolittle Raid—America's First World War II Victory*. New York: Penguin Books, 2002.

North, Oliver, and Joe Musser. *War Stories II: Heroism in the Pacific*. Washington, DC: Regnery, 2004.

Okerstrom, Dennis R. *Dick Cole's War: Doolittle Raider, Hump Pilot, Air Commando*. Columbia: University of Missouri Press, 2015.

Spaulding, G. H., Capt., USN (*Ret.*) "The Doolittle Raid: How America Responded to the Sneak Attack on Pearl Harbor." *Centennial Aviation and Business Journal*, January 2000.

George Nolta has an MBA from UC Berkeley and is an Air Force veteran. He retired from a career of managing the development of new computer systems for Kaiser Aluminum & Chemical Corporation. He lives in Citrus Heights, California, with his wife of sixty-two years—Carol Beebe. After retirement, George developed the hobby of writing articles for the Colusi County Historical Society. He wrote an article about Ellen Lawson—the widow of Maj. Ted Lawson, one of the Doolittle Raiders and author of *Thirty Seconds Over Tokyo*. Ellen liked the article and asked George to write a book about the lives of the Raiders based on her private collection of Raider information and memorabilia.